BOOTSTRAPPING BRONTO

BOOTSTRAPPING BRONTO

The Art of Scaling Your Startup Without Venture Capital

JOE COLOPY

HOUNDSTOOTH
PRESS

BOOTSTRAPPING BRONTO

The Art of Scaling Your Startup Without Venture Capital

FIRST EDITION

ISBN	978-1-5445-4935-4	*Hardcover*
	978-1-5445-4934-7	*Paperback*
	978-1-5445-4933-0	*Ebook*
	978-1-5445-4936-1	*Audiobook*

To Karalyn and our four dinos—Ximena, Xiomara, Xalvador, and Xaviera. Thanks for traveling this startup journey with me. Bronto may be history, but you're my forever herd.

CONTENTS

INTRODUCTION

Click!

The click of the camera rang in a new era for Bronto Software, the company I built with Chaz Felix over the last thirteen years. It was the morning of April 23, 2015. I stood with my team as an independent company for the last time. The night before, I had signed the official documents for Bronto Software to join NetSuite, a publicly traded Silicon Valley-based company, as the largest acquisition in their history. It was also one of the biggest success stories for the region.

The Bronto team celebrating, moments after the acquisition announcement.

It was graduation day. Chaz and I were at our headquarters in Durham, North Carolina. Durham is the home of Duke University. It is one of the three corners of what is affectionately known as the Triangle, a hub for emerging technology companies in the Southeast United States. We went for grand effect to make the official announcement to our employees. We gathered our hundreds of employees onto the lawn of the American Tobacco Campus in Durham for, unbeknownst to them, one last team picture as an independent company.

Seconds before the click, we announced, "Today, we were acquired by one of our strategic partners—NetSuite—for $200 million." At that point, Bronto's long path as a high-growth bootstrapped technology company would end, and our new journey as part of a large publicly traded technology company would begin.

After selling and leaving Bronto, I can now reflect on the experience—what worked, what did not, and what was truly special. Bronto was a high-growth startup in a competitive space that was entirely bootstrapped—that was special, especially in an industry where venture capital is synonymous with startups and often seen as the essential requirement for success.

This book celebrates this alternative funding path of bootstrapping and tells the story of my journey while sharing the lessons learned. Its purpose is not to justify a singular path for building a startup but rather to share the lessons learned along the way—most notably, how a startup can be successful and bootstrapped and how bootstrapping a startup can be a better path for the founder compared to raising venture capital.

Through my years as an entrepreneur, I have come to

realize that many of the assumptions surrounding entrepreneurship, bootstrapping, and venture capital were incomplete and, in many cases, incorrect. In this book, I rethink these assumptions and dispel the myths around venture capital.

I also hope to inspire aspiring entrepreneurs and give them examples, frameworks, and thoughts on how to start, grow, and sell their high-growth startup without venture capital—in other words, how to bootstrap.

I have a unique perspective on this subject. Few bootstrapped startups have had large successful exits. Even fewer entrepreneurs have continuously led such startups, from coding the first line of the product with zero revenue and no employees to signing the legal documents for a multi-hundred-million-dollar acquisition with hundreds of employees across the globe. I have experienced every bump in the road throughout this journey and want to share what I have learned and, more importantly, help others avoid some of the pain that I endured!

As valuable as that experience was, my true education came after leaving Bronto. I learned a lot from building Bronto, but sometimes it is hard to completely understand what went right and what went wrong when you are in the thick of it. In the last ten years, through various ventures, I have met and interviewed hundreds of founders and invested in a healthy fraction of their startups.

I wrote this book to distill and share my learnings from the accumulation of these many experiences to help entrepreneurs who are early in their journey. I have seen many founders commit critical mistakes early in a startup's life, leading to significant ramifications down the road. Hopefully, this book can help entrepreneurs avoid many of these mistakes and build amazingly valuable and impactful companies.

This is the story of my entrepreneurial journey and the lessons learned along the way. Enjoy!

THE ORIGIN STORY

My entrepreneurial life did not start with Bronto. My approach and perspective were forged when I was young by my environment, choices, and experiences. Bronto was my first company, but it was not my first experience jumping into the unknown. Most successful entrepreneurs have had many experiences with healthy doses of grit, resourcefulness, persistence, and curiosity in their past before incorporating a legal entity and calling it a startup. That was certainly true for me.

My personal story helps explain my choices in building Bronto, including why I bootstrapped. Ultimately, this personal story helps entrepreneurs understand which aspects of the Bronto story apply to their situations and which ones are obvious products of my earlier opportunities and challenges.

Now, without further ado, let us get started. And like all stories, we must start at the beginning to tell it best. Here we go.

IN THE BEGINNING

I was born in Akron in the early 1970s. Akron was a great place to grow up, but not a place of glitz and glamor. Akron is in Northeast Ohio, about forty miles south of downtown Cleveland. It is affectionately known as the "Rubber City" because it was the center of rubber production in the early twentieth century, home to major tire manufacturers like Goodyear, Goodrich, and Firestone.

Many famous, notable people were born and raised in Akron. Chrissie Hynde of The Pretenders and both members of The Black Keys attended my high school, Firestone High School, named after the founder of the aforementioned tire company. LeBron James, one of the greatest basketball players ever, also hails from Akron. When I graduated high school, he was four and a half years old, and I am 100 percent confident that I could have beaten him in a game of one-on-one basketball then. After that, his athletic prowess grew while my abilities leveled out.

Akron prides itself as a working-class town with middle-class values. It is not particularly known for technology. Despite this, since my talents were not with basketball and playing hypothetical games against future NBA all-stars, I turned my attention to computers.

FIRST CONTACT

Like many of today's prominent technology entrepreneurs, I was exposed to and embraced computers at a relatively young age. In the early 1980s, when I was in elementary school, it became in vogue for many middle-class households to purchase a home computer.

Atari, Commodore 64, and Texas Instruments were the

popular brands. IBM, Compaq, and other PC varieties were too expensive for the home and usually sold to businesses. Apple computers were expensive but became popular in schools that could afford them.

I was fortunate to have an older half-brother, Bob, who worked at Texas Instruments. For Christmas, while I was in fifth grade, he gave my family the newest model of a Texas Instruments home computer. It was called the TI-99/4A. My parents let us use it under one condition—we could not buy games. The only games we would play would be the games we created ourselves. My three brothers opted out of this challenge. I was inspired. This kicked off a saga of hundreds of hours of learning how to code and initiated my life-changing journey into computers. I started by coding in the BASIC programming language that was popular at the time and spent endless hours in middle school spinning up my versions of karate, spy, and Dungeons & Dragons themed games. I got pretty good at it.

In 1982, my friend David and I started a bulletin board system (BBS) on his home computer. It was called the Commodore Crusader, and we were its pre-teen system operators, or "sysops" for short. BBSes were essentially the websites of the pre-World Wide Web era of the internet. Other computer users would connect to a BBS by calling a phone number with their modem. One user per phone line could log on. In our case, we used David's parents' spare phone line, so it was limited to one user at a time.

Setting up a BBS and toying around with modems was not a common middle school activity, but it was a natural extension for any curious, technically inclined preteen who had too much time on his hands and access to the computers of the day.

EARLY ENTREPRENEURSHIP

As a middle schooler, I was also entrepreneurial. After school, I delivered the *Akron Beacon Journal* newspaper to houses in my adjoining neighborhood and, every winter, sold Christmas trees as part of my Boy Scout troop. Selling Christmas trees during the freezing December nights of Northeast Ohio makes for a hardy kid. That was me. I am still thawing out!

My entrepreneurial activities continued during the school year. I made and sold Dungeons & Dragons modules to classmates during my classes. Later, I illicitly sold one-cent Pal gum to my nearby seatmates for five cents, stealthily dealing them out of my backpack while my teacher was not paying attention. Wisely, I shut down that endeavor before getting caught when my teachers started trying to pinpoint the source of the increased gum chewing. If I had grown up in a different family with a different disposition, I might have been a drug dealer. I like to think that I would have made a great one.

LEAVING HOME

In the fall of 1985, I started attending Firestone High School and focused on academics, clubs, and athletics. I did not spend too much time using computers other than typing English papers or solving math problems. I was too busy. However, this focus and busyness paid off, and I was fortunate enough to get admitted to Harvard University. At Harvard, I studied computer science and economics. In hindsight, I had a mediocre academic career in college. I was more of an aspiring entrepreneur than a budding academic—I always erred toward doing and building instead of researching and writing.

After graduation, I wanted to try something different. I was confident in my ability to support myself when I needed to. I have always been very resourceful and motivated. Also, since I was very good with computers, an in-demand skill even back then, I did not think I would have problems getting a job when I wanted one. I had student debt, but you only see possibilities when you are young and capable. I wanted to try something that would be difficult to do when I was older. I wanted to see more of the world.

I had spent my life in Ohio and only first left the country on road trips to Canada while I was in college. So, after graduating, to see the bigger world, I joined the US Peace Corps. Next thing I knew, I was flying off to Seychelles in late 1993. Seychelles is an interesting faraway place and seems like the French-culture islands in the Caribbean. But in actuality, Seychelles is a small island country in the Indian Ocean a thousand miles off the east coast of Africa and about 400 miles north of Madagascar. In essence, I went to the other side of the world.

8800 MILES AWAY

I had a unique assignment in Seychelles. I taught computer science to the country's best and brightest at its School of Humanities and Science. The country only had a population of 75,000, but the best and brightest high schoolers kept me on my toes.

I found my days to be an eclectic blend of teaching younger high school students about spreadsheets and the older high school students A-Level Computing, the rough British equivalent of the College Board's Advanced Placement course in the US. At home, I whittled away the hours boiling water to sanitize for drinking and listening to the country's one radio station rotate between reggae tunes and country western hits of a different era. It was so weird, and I loved it.

Most importantly, I learned how to teach. I learned how to organize and articulate my ideas. I learned how to excite and energize groups of young people. I was an enthusiastic young teacher in a very traditional educational system. I like to think that my students enjoyed it as much as I did. At the very least, I made it memorable.

Most Americans have never heard of Seychelles, much less could find it on a map. I certainly couldn't before I was assigned to go there. It was an adventure, and I enjoyed my two years there. After that experience, my girlfriend Karalyn, whom I met in college and later married, and I backpacked through East Africa for several months, sharing one large backpack and a minuscule daily budget. In early 1996, after a short stint back in the US, we embarked on another venture. We found teaching jobs at a new private school in Guayaquil, Ecuador. This time, however, our adventurous spirit got the better of us.

An embezzlement scandal by one of its founders led to a quickly deteriorating financial situation at the school. A few months later, the paychecks became more sporadic. In an even more bizarre turn of events, the embezzling co-founder sent gunmen to the school to collect money from the other co-founder, the school's president. I believed the president to be honest but incompetent. This led to him and his family going on the run and hiding in the hills and valleys of Ecuador. Then, a local judge was bribed to issue warrants for the arrest of the president and his family. It was wild and more than what Karalyn and I had signed up for.

So, we cut our Ecuador teaching tenure short and returned to the United States about four months later.

ONWARD TO NORTH CAROLINA

After that adventure, we decided to take a break from international travel. In 1996, the magazine *US News & World Report* listed the Triangle—the Raleigh–Durham area of North Carolina—as one of the best places to live. With its great reputation, the area seemed worth trying out. The place was warmer and had a stronger economy than Northeast Ohio or Northern New Jersey, where Karalyn hailed from. Plus, the area had strong universities, and I planned to start business school in a few years. At the very least, we figured our next adventure of moving to North Carolina would not include embezzlement or roaming gunmen.

In July 1996, we moved to Durham, North Carolina, and soon found an affordable apartment near Duke University to move into. Karalyn found a research job at the Research Triangle Institute, a large regional think tank. I found a job as a trainer at a small computer training outfit in the area. Life was good. We moved to nearby Chapel Hill the following year, and I soon started a two-year MBA program at the University of North Carolina.

Starting an MBA program provided a few advantages. First, I could continue to defer my undergraduate student loans. Second, the program helped me transition from being a teacher to preparing for a respectable, upstanding corporate job.

As is customary in business school, I had a summer internship between my first and second year of school. I spent my internship working at Dell Computer in Austin,

Texas. Dell had the highest-flying stock in the 1990s, so it was an exciting place to be. Even in those early days, Dell was a large company with tens of thousands of employees. Also, Dell was fundamentally a hardware company whose success and failure were dictated by coordinating supply chains and maximizing thin margins.

I enjoyed different things. I liked the creativity and leverage of the software and internet space. Also, I liked living in the Triangle more than in Austin. Both regions are similar in that they contain state capitals and are progressive political islands within more conservative states. Finally, they both have a strong academic and tech culture.

My experience at Dell also helped me realize I had zero interest in a respectable, upstanding corporate job. I was more entrepreneurial than that. I thrived on the ambiguity and adventure of trying something new and different. It was the late 1990s, in the heart of what we would later realize was the dot-com bubble, so the stars aligned well for me to begin a different type of search.

THE STARTUP SEARCH

When I returned for my second year of business school, I focused on finding a startup to join—someplace where I could learn a little bit about what a successful startup looks like before embarking on building my own, not knowing when and what that would be.

In the spring of 1999, I hustled my way into a little company based in Durham that had a foothold in the not-well-understood space of Linux and open-source software. The startup was high-profile in the technology industry but still very small.

My hustle plan was twofold. First, my friends and I filmed a video explaining why I wanted to work there. I FedEx-ed it on a DVD to the CEO. I had heard that FedEx-ing a package was better than mailing one because it bypassed their executive assistant, who acted as their corporate gate-keeper. Pro tip: that worked for me and may work for you!

The main part of the video was lame, but the blooper reel at the end was a big hit. Digital videos were challenging to create in 1999, so my effort stood out. Today, you can watch the video online.[1] Second, I organized a time for the CEO to speak at my school, with over a hundred of my fellow MBA classmates attending. The CEO was impressed.

My plan worked and I joined the company as an intern while in school and soon after transitioned into full-time online marketing manager. That role relied on a nice mix of early internet experiences and newfound marketing skills.

The company had fewer than a hundred employees when I joined. About a year later, the company grew to more than 500 employees and went public, achieving—at the time—the eighth biggest, first-day gain in Wall Street history. And many years later, in 2019, this company—Red Hat—was acquired by IBM for $34 billion—IBM's largest-ever acquisition. And just like that, this once little company became the generational success story of the Triangle.

It was a crazy year working there. However, after that time, I decided that I had learned enough and that it was time to take some winnings from the IPO to craft my own startup. These winnings came from selling the small allocation of stock options I received when I started full time. The company also offered employees the opportunity to buy "friends and family" shares at pre-IPO prices. During the dot-com boom, friends and family stock purchase programs were popular.[2] I bought all I could, and that bet paid off when I sold them less than a year later. These winnings provided the financial cushion that I needed to get started.

In July 2000, after a particularly stressful day at work, I came home and convinced Karalyn to go to the theater and see that summer's surprise hit, *Big Momma's House*, where Martin Lawrence goes undercover as a grandmother to solve a murder case. Hilarity ensued!

After the movie, Karalyn and I discussed my resignation from Red Hat and starting my own venture. She knew I was increasingly unhappy and bored at Red Hat, and I had an insatiable itch to pave my own path. Both Karalyn and I are frugal, and with the paycheck and health benefits from her job, and our new little nest egg, we could make this work.

The next day, I resigned from Red Hat, and in a few short weeks, my entrepreneurial journey began. I was determined to create the next great thing. The next great thing would be Bronto...eventually.

THE BRONTO JOURNEY

Bronto was officially incorporated as BrontoMail Inc. on May 15, 2002, twenty-two months after I left my job at Red Hat. Those were a hard twenty-two months. I did not have a brilliant idea when I left, so I spent the ensuing time experimenting with ideas, learning web programming, and developing an early predecessor to Bronto. That predecessor was called DatabaseApp.

DatabaseApp was a web-based database service where customers could use easy tools to store, manipulate, and report on information online. The product was great but had one major flaw—no one knew about it, much less used it. No customers meant no business.

By the end of 2001, DatabaseApp was going nowhere, and my day-in-day-out life of coding and making no money was getting old. I was getting discouraged, and the excitement of embarking on my own had long since worn off. Also, Karalyn and I were expecting our first baby in six months, so the stakes had gone up. They say, "Necessity is the mother of invention." At this point, I had a lot of necessity and was ready for some invention.

As a last-ditch effort, I simplified the product and refocused it around one customer need—sending email newsletters. Eureka! BrontoMail was born a few weeks later, in January 2002.

BrontoMail was a simple email newsletter product for small businesses. I named it after my childhood love for dinosaurs and an early sense of branding. The name set the tone for Bronto to be a different kind of company. I did not want to give this company a typical tech name, and I did not want the brand to sound generic. Of course, naming the company after a Brontosaurus, from one perspective, was a terrible idea for a high-growth tech company. The Brontosaurus was notoriously big, slow, and had a brain the size of a pea. Also, it turns out that the Brontosaurus—which I learned about as a child—likely never even existed.

During the Great Dinosaur Rush of the late 1800s, a paleontologist put the wrong head on another dinosaur, Apatosaurus, and erroneously labeled it as a Brontosaurus. Sometime after I was a curious second grader, this mistake became known, and the Brontosaurus was stripped of its legitimacy. I painfully learned this from my niece a few years after starting the company. At the time, she was nine years old and told me this with all the confidence that nine-year-olds tend to have about the world.

Fortunately, in 2015, right around the time the company was sold, the Brontosaurus was "re-dinosaured" when a study unexpectedly found evidence that Brontosaurus was distinct all along. I can only imagine that those two events might be connected.

Despite this controversy, Bronto became a great name for the company. Because of its quirky and questionable backstory, the dinosaur name embodied the company's humility in humanizing technology and software. Bronto and its employees had personalities, and the name reflected that. It set the tone for what Bronto would become.

BARTERED BETAS

I crafted two product-for-advertising barter arrangements with small local email newsletter publishers to gain early momentum. I let them use the product for free in exchange for advertising in their newsletters. These arrangements were helpful in two ways. First, I received useful feedback from them using the product, which was critical in helping me refine it. Second, this early advertising generated inquiries from prospective customers. These efforts soon led to my first paying customer. Concurrently, Chaz Felix joined as a co-founder in April 2002 to accelerate these efforts. We incorporated the business as BrontoMail, Inc. on May 15, 2002. Then we were off to the races...finally!

We ended the first year with $17,000 in revenue. We did this by selling subscriptions for our simple newsletter product to small businesses in the area. Toward the end of the year, we hired a few college interns from the University of

North Carolina to help, and early the following year, we hired a full-time support person to handle inbound product questions from existing customers. We forwent salaries for another eighteen months and reinvested everything we could to grow the business.

Of course, $17,000 does not sound like very much, but BrontoMail was what one would later describe as a software-as-a-service ("SaaS") business. This means that we were being paid recurringly instead of up front. So, although we only made $17,000 in 2002, BrontoMail's revenue run rate month after month was much higher and growing. By December, our effective annualized revenue run rate would have put us on track for roughly two or three times that total number. We had the beginning of a very real company.

We continued to grow in 2003 and to live and operate meagerly. By the end of our second year, we rebranded the company as Bronto Software after acquiring the domain name bronto.com, and we ended with revenues of roughly $170,000, ten times the year before. The years of work building a strong foundation for the product and company were finally paying off.

Revenue grew over the years. We evolved the product and focused the company on online retailers because we knew that email marketing was more of a revenue generator for them versus a nice-to-have for the various small business verticals that we had previously sold to. That strategy worked and the revenue followed.

BABY STEPS TO SCALE

By 2010, we had grown beyond $10 million in annual revenue, and we opened offices outside of Durham to better tackle other parts of the world and service larger companies within the US. We opened small sales and services offices in London (UK), Sydney (Australia), New York, and Los Angeles in the following years.

There were many ups and downs from our inception through the next thirteen years. It was hard. We were on a constant drumbeat of building, hiring, and iterating. The product got more sophisticated, especially when we grew large enough to hire full-time software engineers. We invested in marketing, acquired more customers, and expanded our physical offices for our ever-growing team. In hindsight, the journey might have seemed straightforward, but at the time, it felt like two steps forward and one step back. We were always moving the goalposts of success forward such that we never felt we could rest on our laurels.

By 2015, our annual revenue had grown to over $40 million, and we were able to achieve that without taking on any outside investors. Then we changed it up. In April 2015, we agreed to sell Bronto to NetSuite, a Silicon Valley-based cloud-based financial software company. NetSuite was acquired by tech behemoth Oracle in 2016. Now, Bronto's spirit lives on through more than 300 folks working for Oracle.

While many high-growth tech startups follow a similar trajectory of being acquired or going public, Bronto had a unique path because our journey was entirely bootstrapped. We did not receive outside financial investment from venture capitalists, angel investors, or wealthy friends and family. We invested tremendous time and persistence—otherwise known as sweat equity—but little financial capital.

It is rare for high-growth technology companies to achieve this scale while being entirely bootstrapped. Most startups that reached our size would have raised millions in venture capital ("VC") investments to get there. Because of this, we evolved differently throughout our journey. This book captures some of those insights from the journey and hopefully explains an alternative to the traditional VC path by sharing the pros (and cons) of bootstrapping a high-growth company based on my own experience in starting, scaling, and selling Bronto.

THE SILICON VALLEY MODEL

Silicon Valley is a twenty-five-mile stretch of technology parks and offices around California's San Francisco Bay. Over the years, this area has produced as much economic value as many industrialized countries, making the United States the wealthiest nation in human history.

Silicon Valley's importance parallels the importance of Florence in the Italian Renaissance. The Italian Renaissance was a period of history in the fifteenth and sixteenth centuries where Italian culture spread from Florence, Italy, across Europe. Silicon Valley has been the Florence of modern-age technology for the last fifty years.

Silicon Valley is synonymous with the titans of the technology space and their companies—like Steve Jobs and Apple, Mark Zuckerberg and Facebook, Larry Ellison and Oracle, and many more.

Venture capitalist firms provided the capital and expertise to fund these startups to their dominant positions. A handful of the region's top VC firms anointed these tech behemoths.

- Sequoia Capital was founded in the early 1970s and funded Apple, Cisco, Google, and many other recognizable names.
- Accel was founded in 1993 and funded Facebook, Dropbox, and Spotify, among many others.
- Andreessen Horowitz, also called a16z,[3] was co-founded by Marc Andreessen[4] in 2009. His firm funded top technology companies like Slack, Airbnb, GitHub, and Pinterest.

Because of these numerous successes, venture capital is clustered around Silicon Valley and the Bay Area. Roughly 40 percent of venture capital invested dollars in the United States hail from that area.[5] Silicon Valley is famous for a reason!

However, venture capital is not required for every high-growth tech startup to be successful. And successful venture capital returns do not necessarily equal success for the entrepreneur.

Because so much venture capital comes from Silicon Valley, this investing style has become synonymous with the region. Given this, I find it best to think of venture capital more as a business model embodied in Silicon Valley. Let us simply call it the "Silicon Valley Model."

VENTURE CAPITAL EXPLAINED

Silicon Valley, the technology industry, and venture capital have been intertwined for the last fifty years. Let us dig into what venture capital is and how it works.

In the simplest form, venture capital is financing that investors provide to startups they believe to have exceptional growth potential. It is referred to as a "venture" because the investment thesis is often based on the company's ability to create a new product and enter a new market with a unique business model.

This is different from how traditional banks assess the riskiness of a loan for a small business. Banks assess risk by looking at existing assets—often serving as collateral—and measuring cash flow. Venture capitalists assess founder talent, product potential, and market opportunity—this is fuzzier and more speculative than what banks do.

Venture capital firms are investment firms that are organized differently than software companies. These firms raise capital from other investors. These investors are traditionally university endowments, pension funds, and very wealthy individuals. These investors are called limited partners, or LPs for short. Their money is organized into a fund by the VC firm with rules governing what and how that money is invested. This includes a fund thesis.

A fund thesis defines the strategy by which the fund makes money for its LPs. Typically, it defines the stage, geography and focus of investments, as well as how the VC firm differentiates itself from other investment funds. Their target companies may be all early-stage, late-stage biotech, or they may seek many other potential strategies.

Funds also have a fund life, which is typically ten years. The venture capitalist finds and invests in target companies for the first half of the fund's life and then reaps the rewards for its investors from selling them in the back half for more than they invested.

Venture capitalists make money from their funds in two ways. First, their LPs pay an annual management fee for the venture capitalists to research potential investments to deploy this capital. This is similar to an annual fee that might be paid to invest in an S&P 500 mutual fund. But the fee is higher since investing in the public market is easy, and investing in unknown small private companies is hard and requires more work and expertise. This management fee pays the venture capitalists' salary, office rent, travel expenses, etc. In short, the money keeps the lights on. Typically, venture capital funds charge a 2 percent annual fee on the invested capital.

THE CARRY CALCULUS

The more significant way venture capitalists make money is through the carried interest, or more simply referred to as "carry." This is the upside. Carry is the share of the profits from selling an investment. Most funds have a 20 percent carry, but it can sometimes run higher. Funds are often described as having "two and twenty" terms. This means 2 percent in annual fees and 20 percent carry to the venture capitalist. Let us go through an example.

Imagine Jessica is a venture capitalist, and she invests in a flashy new startup called SaurusAI. SaurusAI is an early-stage startup that develops and sells artificial intelligence avatars of dinosaurs to reinvent early childhood education. The initial investment is $1 million for 20 percent of the startup. SaurusAI grows amazingly, and five years later, it is sold to Google for $500 million, without any additional rounds of investment—which is unlikely but possible.

Jessica's $1 million investment is now worth $100 million, or 20 percent of the $500 million sale price. I am simplifying the math here, but let us roll with it and see how the money rolls back to Jessica, her venture capital fund, and her fund's LPs.

There is a $99 million gain from her $1 million investment. What happens now? How is the money distributed? Venture capitalists refer to this as the distribution waterfall.[6] The exact method can vary, but generally it works something like this:

- The annual fees are first paid back to the fund's investors. A 2 percent annual fee on a $1 million investment equals $20,000. Over the five years, the aggregate fees are $100,000.
- The gain from the investment is $99 million. (i.e., $100 million minus $1 million initial investment minus $100,000 in fees). According to the fund's terms, the venture capital firm receives 20 percent of the gain as carry. The remaining 80 percent is distributed to the investors. Jessica's venture capital firm yields almost $20 million (i.e., 20 percent of $99 million gain). The funds' investors receive the other 80 percent of the gain, which is almost $80 million.
- The venture capital carry is split within the firm, with the general partners receiving most of the carry. Jessica is one of three general partners (GPs) in her firm, and she is getting a fourth of the distribution. In her firm, the other two quarters go to the other GPs, and the remaining fourth is split between the rest of the investment team, operating partners, and advisors.
- Jessica receives almost $5 million (i.e., 25 percent of a nearly $20 million distribution to the firm). Not bad! Somewhat controversially, due to a 2002 law, the US tax code considers this type of gain as long-term capital gains versus income.[7] This means she will be taxed on that gain at about half the rate of what she would be if it were considered income on her tax return.

With the sale, Jessica is happy. Her investors are happy. SaurusAI founders are happy too. Everyone wins. Media outlets often simplify this story—however, the reality is usually more nuanced and challenging.

THE CHALLENGES

Venture capital is best applied to startups introducing a new product or market. There is a high-risk, high-return aspect to it. The chance of failure is high. The venture capitalists promise that they can better assess risk than their investors can on their own. They invest in a portfolio of these startups and ideally yield above-market returns. Most of their portfolio's startups will fail. Some will do okay. One may do incredibly well and return so much capital that it outweighs the other losses. The return dynamic is also called the "power law."[8] In our earlier example, this might have been the case with Jessica's investment into SaurusAI. The return of SaurusAI was exceptional.

Power law says that a small thing can disproportionately influence everything else. With venture investing, an investment in one company can have such outlier results that it completely outweighs in a positive sense the negligible returns from the others. This is the basis of the venture capital model, and this investing style has become synonymous with Silicon Valley. It is understandable why. The largest technology companies were born from this model, and the financial returns for early investors from these "home runs" have been incredible. Here are some examples:

- In 2004, Peter Thiel, the co-founder of PayPal, invested $500,000 in Facebook for 10 percent of the company.

When Facebook did its initial public offering (IPO) in 2012, Peter sold most of his shares for over $1 billion.

- In 2011, Sequoia Capital invested $8 million in WhatsApp, a social media company. After following on with an additional investment of $52 million, WhatsApp was acquired by Facebook in 2014 for $22 billion.[9] That is billion with a "b"!
- In 2012, Lightspeed Venture Partners invested $8 million into Snap, a social media company. Its initial investment was worth $2 billion when Snap did its IPO five years later.

These exceptional stories provided tremendous returns for these venture capital firms, their LPs, and, of course, the founders of the invested startups. But, just like how every high school basketball player is not going to the NBA, LeBron James, my fellow Akronite, is the exception, not the rule.

Successes make for great headlines. But the headlines are the exceptions, and the simplified press-friendly hype stories do not truly capture the experience from the entrepreneur's perspective.

The average fund results illustrate this disconnect. The top quartile of funds returned over 20 percent a year over the last ten years, but the median return for funds is closer to 10 percent. This return is comparable to that of a run-of-the-mill mutual fund but with more risk and far less liquidity.[10]

MISMATCHED INCENTIVES

The "haves and have-nots" nature of venture capital returns and the power law rules affect the entrepreneur. It is a "swing for the fences" model. And that financing model does not necessarily (and usually does not) work for most startup founders. It creates a "growth at all costs" mentality as investors seek power law returns. On the one hand, pressure can be invaluable in pushing a startup to greatness. It can also push unrealistic goals and destroy startups prematurely.

There is an expression in the venture capital community of finding investments that will "make the fund." This is when one investment does so well and returns so much capital that its gain far outweighs the good, mediocre, or poor returns from the other investments in the portfolio. Often, this ratio is one to nine—one amazing investment makes up for the nine.

This portfolio strategy makes sense for a venture capitalist and the investors in their fund. But this dynamic is not good if you are one of the other invested startups, especially if your startup was previously doing well. Entrepreneurs focus on one company at a time. Venture capitalists focus on many. This mismatch of incentives can cause problems—what is best for the startup? What is best for the investor? Incentives do not always align.

Another mismatch of incentives is between fund size, management fees, and the need to deploy capital. It is more lucrative for a venture capital firm to receive 2 percent per year in management fees from a $1 billion fund than a $10 million fund. The annual management fee for a $10 million fund would be $200,000. That sounds like a lot of money until one puts together the costs of running a fund between salaries, travel, office, etc. No one is getting rich on the management fees from a $10 million fund.

Things are different with a $1 billion fund. The management fees would be $20 million per year. The team needed to invest and support a $1 billion fund is larger than that required by a $10 million fund, but it is not a hundred times the size. There are economies of scale. Because of this, most fund managers have an incentive to grow their fund sizes.

Funds are obligated to invest this capital. Often, this gives them the incentive to make fewer larger investments instead of more of them. It requires less time to make fewer, larger investments than more, smaller ones. Human time and effort are the constraining factors. This can create an incentive to invest more money into individual startups than makes sense. Whereas, for the startup, the founder wants the appropriate amount of investment because more investment dilutes their ownership in their startup.

MO MONEY, MO PROBLEMS

Venture capital is not free money. Entrepreneurs exchange ownership in their startups for investment. When entrepreneurs take more money than they can (or should) use, the founders' ownership gets diluted, and they own less of the company. Of course, the exchange works out great if the money is used efficiently. But that is not always the case. The danger is that the motivation behind the investment can be that the venture capitalists need to deploy capital from the fund, rather than meeting—and not exceeding—the funding needs of the startup. Overfunding startups is a real problem.

The Notorious B.I.G., a long-deceased 1990s rap star, wrote the song, "Mo Money Mo Problems." Too much money can insulate entrepreneurs from hearing and addressing the startup's problems—the kinks that need to be worked out. It is akin to turning up the radio while driving down the road to drown out the noise of your car engine clanking. No good comes out of that.

The Silicon Valley Model of venture capital has made many investors and founders wildly successful. Success attracts money, and this money needs a home. Large institutions like university endowments and pensions are sources of that money. These groups allot a small percentage of their portfolio into venture capital. This small percentage can be significant when referring to large investors—like Harvard University's $38 billion endowment or California's Public Employees' Retirement System (CalPERS) $469 billion pension fund.

These dynamics create more pressure for venture capitalists to fund startups too early in their lifecycle and with too much funding than is ideal for their founders, teams, and customers.

These are some of the land mines that entrepreneurs should be aware of as they create impactful and valuable startups. Fortunately, venture capital funding is not the only path.

Enter "The Bootstrap Model."

THE BOOTSTRAP MODEL

Bootstrapping is an alternative to venture capital and the Silicon Valley Model for growing startups. These startups can be as successful as venture capital-funded startups and often have more staying power.

Funding strategy is not a simple preference. There are many considerations with various pros and cons. Your choice of model depends on several factors—like the entrepreneur's track record, circumstances, or propensity, and the startup's business model, industry, and ownership structure. Let us dig into them.

TRACK RECORD

I know we are focusing on bootstrapping but bear with me as I pull focus for a moment—I promise you will see why—to highlight what a venture capitalist wants. When a venture capitalist (or anyone) invests in a very early-stage startup, the investor bets on the founder more than anything. There are plenty of great markets and great products. Founder hustle, drive, and talent get ideas off the ground. Ideas are plentiful. Founders who turn ideas into something big are rare. These are the kind of founders that investors are looking for.

Great investors know that past performance is often the best predictor of future success. This is particularly true in high-risk environments with plenty of unknowns. They bet on familiar patterns of success. These investors are pattern recognizers. They are looking for past successes in other arenas. These past successes might mean the entrepreneur is a recent computer science graduate of a prestigious university. Why? This was the founder profile behind startup high-flyers like Google, Amazon, and others. Those investors in those startups did great, so other investors want similar successes, so they follow the herd and look for that story again. It is not a perfect system, but it is a harsh reality that most first-time entrepreneurs must face.

The reality is also that most entrepreneurs are first-time founders and do not have a storybook background, so venture capitalists often overlook their startups. Chasing venture capital early on in a startup's life is time-consuming. Usually, first-time entrepreneurs without a strong track record have a tough time getting startups funded. These entrepreneurs should focus on bootstrapping their business, building a great product, and acquiring customers.

Paying customers are what makes for a great business—not marquee investors. This makes being successful as an entrepreneur more accessible for everyone, regardless of your educational pedigree and background.

CIRCUMSTANCES

Time and place circumstances also influence the appropriate funding path. As an example, I started Bronto Software in the aftermath of the dot-com bust, circa the early 2000s. Those were dark times for all technology companies. The venture capital spigot for startups had gone from uncontrollably gushing to a mere trickle. With each new day, news headlines rattled off the demise of another crumbling startup. Venture capital funds were having dismal returns. It was doom and gloom in the technology industry.

In 2001, a neighbor asked me what I was working on day after day in my house. I told him about DatabaseApp, my first internet-based product. He replied, "Isn't this internet thing over?" Of course, it was not. Facebook was still years away from even being a tap on Mark Zuckerberg's keyboard.

Chaz and I did not seek venture capital at Bronto, which was not a hard decision in the early days since venture capital was difficult to get in those poor market conditions. Venture capital had gone on life support after years of unbridled activity. This ended up being a great benefit to us. The plus of this dismal investment climate was the ability to focus. We could focus on getting customers and improving the product versus chasing investors. As first-time founders, chasing investors likely would have been time-consuming and yielded very little.

Geography is another circumstance that matters. Even with the prevalence of remote work and instant communications, thirty-seven miles is the average distance between a startup and its lead investor.[11] Only thirty-seven miles! And that distance has not varied much in many years.[12] This statistic reinforces the connection between investors and invested startups within a region. This limited distance is one of the reasons why investors and entrepreneurs tend to clump in a particular geographic area. In Q2 of 2024, almost 35 percent of venture capital was deployed in the Bay Area.[13] Silicon Valley and the surrounding area continue to be where most venture capital dollars flow.

Venture capital is less prevalent in secondary markets like Raleigh–Durham, North Carolina, than in tech hotspots like Silicon Valley. Most would see this as bad. I do not. In smaller markets, it is easier to see alternatives and not confuse venture capital as the one and only way to fund a startup. Does a fish know it is in water? Outside that fishbowl, assessing the alternatives and deciding the best path can be easier.

PROPENSITY

Building a startup is an exercise in mental fortitude. It is very challenging, regardless of the funding model. However, for entrepreneurs wired to build, the experience can be enriching and worthwhile. One funny quip says: *Entrepreneurs are the only people who work eighty hours a week to avoid working forty*. Entrepreneurs, especially bootstrapped ones, must have a certain propensity to be successful. This is particularly true for bootstrapped entrepreneurs focused on spending sweat equity rather than seeking equity investors.

Venture capital is rocket fuel for startups. It helps startups get where they are going faster. The challenge is ensuring the startups are going in the right direction when the fuel starts burning. Adjusting direction once they get going is very hard. If you shoot a rocket, it will go somewhere fast. Hopefully, the rocket zooms up into the sky instead of careening into the side of the house.

Bootstrapped startups are different. The speed of growth is more under the entrepreneur's control. Time fuels these startups. This time can help the entrepreneur build a solid platform to grow from and pay tremendous long-term dividends. This is hard to accomplish if the startup is racing at an unsustainable pace.

The Bronto experience was a marathon, not a sprint. By 2004, Bronto generated over $1 million in revenue per year. That year, Chaz and I paid ourselves a little over $50,000 per year. That was roughly four years after I left my steady paycheck at Red Hat, earning a comparable amount.

By 2005, we doubled our revenue and upped our paychecks to $80,000 per year. The growth continued. The pace of Bronto and the size of my paycheck grew even more as the years passed.

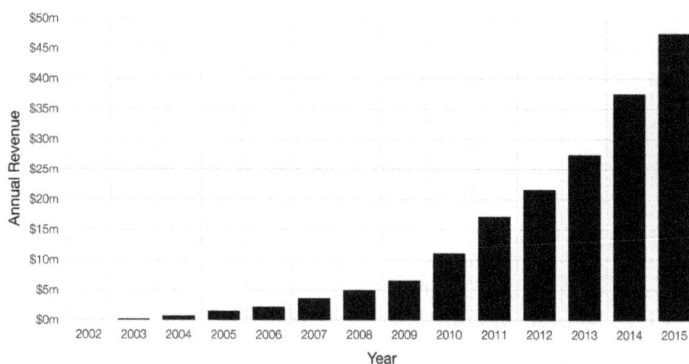

Bronto's annual revenue from 2002 to 2015

A more aggressive version of this type of growth is often described as hockey stick growth. This is where the growth of the startup, whether in revenue, users, or whatever metric, follows the path of the hockey stick. The blade represents the early years when growth is negligible. The main part of the stick represents when growth shoots up—up and to the right, as chart-loving startup enthusiasts love saying.

In a bootstrapped business, the blade years are particularly long because there is no additional funding to jump ahead. Bootstrapped entrepreneurs should be prepared. These years are hard. Bootstrapping a startup takes longer than growing a venture-backed one, but the result can be better for the entrepreneur.

BUSINESS MODEL

A business model is "a company's plan for making a profit. It identifies the products or services the business plans to sell, its identified target market, and any anticipated expenses."[14] Startups have different kinds of business models.

Some businesses require a heavy investment before getting to the starting line. For example, manufacturing businesses need investment to build up inventory of physical products and purchase machinery. In these cases, these businesses seek loans to purchase the raw materials and machinery because these purchases require more capital than the business has. They will repay the loan from the revenue on selling the finished products.

The return on capital is more straightforward—borrow $1 million to invest in machinery to press bricks, sell them for a profit, and use some of the profit to repay the debt. Without significant investment, the business is going nowhere. Bricks are not pressed with hopes and dreams! These types of businesses can be great, but fundamental attributes require them to be bootstrapped in a certain way.

Service businesses are different. They look like, *I am a*

human. I do this service for you. You pay me for that service. They are very common—everything from web design firms to beauty salons falls into this category. The revenue model is usually based on "time and materials." One of the challenges with service businesses is that they require people to grow. More services require more people and hence more expense. The initial cash flow can be quick but the gross margin can be low.

Gross margin is the difference in revenue and cost to deliver an offering to a customer. The cost of delivering another widget is negligible in software-based product companies, so the gross margin can be very high. The gross margin is lower for service businesses because the cost of delivering more service is not negligible. The service requires humans to do something, and humans are expensive.

Service businesses, however, can be a great first step to starting a product business. Consider this: run a service company doing a specific type of work for clients, notice a recurring need that would be great to productize, siphon some of your service profit to develop a product and try it on your existing base of customers, and finally, continue to invest the excess service profit to develop the product.

If all goes well, the more profitable product business soon outstrips the service business until it makes sense to spin it out and/or shut down the service business.

Starting a service business can be a great option if you are unsure how to bootstrap a product company. But remember that it can be challenging to shift your style of operating from one to the other. Many entrepreneurs and their companies struggle to make this transition and never truly build a high gross margin product business. Changing styles is hard.

CASH FLOW & PRICING

"Cash is king" is a common saying in the startup world. This saying inspires another business model consideration: the nature of cash flow or, more simply, time-to-cash. Time-to-cash is how long it takes to sell to a customer and have them pay; at least initially, it affects what kind of customers the startup focuses on. The pro of having large customers is that they can pay a lot. But, the con, which ends up being much worse, is that they can take a long time to sell to, and they often pay slowly.

Most startups have little financial cushion, so slow-selling and slow-paying can be deadly. You cannot eat accounts receivables! Also, startups with a small number of large customers risk "having too many eggs in one basket." And they are more vulnerable to customer attrition or other issues than a startup with many small customers. In business jargon speak, they would be said to have a highly fragmented customer base.

The price point of the product sold to the customer is a key piece of the business model. Pricing can start low to build another base of easier-to-acquire customers and move up with time. Prices can shift up as the product improves and becomes established. As a startup's revenue increases, it is better positioned to handle larger customers and manage revenue swings.

In Bronto's early years, our average customer paid us $1800 per year. Our customers were small businesses that could quickly assess our product and purchase it. They primarily paid up front by credit card, too. These positive attributes let Bronto grow when it was small and had limited financial resources. Quick buying and paying customers gave us good predictability in our revenue and made it easier to plan our growth and manage our costs. But our price did not stay constant.

By 2015, Bronto's average customer value (ACV) was $40,000 per year, with our largest customers paying us over $1 million annually. This was very different from the $1800 per year price point that we had when we began. But, in the later stages, this was manageable since we could weather swings in payment schedules from enterprise customers.

The nature of the business model is an important consideration when bootstrapping. This is especially true in the early stages of a startup's journey when there is less financial wiggle room.

OWNERSHIP

The ownership structure is one of the most obvious differences between a bootstrapped and a venture-backed startup. This difference can result in dramatically different financial returns when the startup is sold. Entrepreneurs need to understand the economic trade-offs when receiving a venture capital investment. Here is a walkthrough of a typical investment journey with venture capital.

Venture capital is usually a multiple-round affair, especially if you raise money early in your startup's lifecycle. The goal of a venture capitalist is to fund your startup, see great growth, and continue to fund it until it is much bigger, and everyone involved sees a great return from a sale. Typically, startups on the venture track raise money every twelve to eighteen months.

The rule of thumb is that investors will own an additional 20 to 25 percent of equity in the startup with each fundraising round. The entrepreneur is diluted with each new round. This makes sense if the startup increases in value at a higher rate than the dilution rate. If the overall size of the "pie" increases enough, then a smaller percentage size is objectively larger. If not, this is a losing proposition for the entrepreneur.

Let us put some middle school math around it. The Founder Dilution Equation looks like this:

$$\textbf{Founder's Ownership} = (75\%)^n$$

75% is the founder team's ownership after a typical venture capital investment round.

n is the number of financing rounds.

The Founder Dilution Equation

Let us apply the Founder Dilution Equation to SaurusAI's investment journey. Enter Jessica, our friendly neighborhood venture capitalist. She values SaurusAI at a $4 million pre-money valuation. Pre-money valuation is how much the startup is worth before investing. She invests $1 million in exchange for 25 percent of the startup. Sarah is the founder, and after the investment, she will use the new capital to hire two software engineers and a salesperson. Plus, she will spend more on marketing. Things are going well. SaurusAI lands some paying customers.

Imagine SaurusAI raises capital again eighteen months later. Sarah feeds that new money into sales and marketing to grow SaurusAI even faster. It works! SaurusAI has more customers and more revenue. SaurusAI is more valuable, but the real question is—did SaurusAI grow fast enough to justify the two rounds of dilution? Is Sarah financially better off? This is the great quandary. Often, the answer is no. The financial outcomes of the entrepreneur Sarah and the investor Jessica can be very different, too. The investment can be a solid outcome for the investors but a so-so one for the entrepreneur. Sarah often would have been better off financially by bootstrapping slowly and selling her smaller, more founder-owned startup.

Dilution matters. Even if a venture-backed startup is fortunate enough to have an initial public offering (IPO), the founder's return can be less than one might expect. On average, the founders collectively own about 15 percent of their startup at the time of an IPO.[15] This can be great. Besides, 15 percent of a billion dollars is $150 million and nothing to sneeze at. This is when everything goes well. Sadly, that is not always the story. The founder might have had a higher likelihood of selling their bootstrapped startup for more than $150 million and do even better.

Let us apply the Founder Dilution Equation to SaurusAI. Say SaurusAI takes the venture capital path and is acquired after six investment rounds. Sarah now owns roughly 18 percent of her startup. This is calculated with a little math by solving for 75 percent set to the sixth power.

This dilution does not include the creation of the initial option pool for employees and its replenishment over time. In this simple example, Sarah would receive almost $180 million. That is nothing to sneeze at but is her selling for $1 billion with venture capital more likely than $180 million without? Maybe. Maybe not. That is the question that all founders should wrestle with.

CONTROL

Bootstrapped entrepreneurs have a tremendous amount of control over their startups. This can be a mixed blessing. Investors hold you accountable. They can help you double-think through your plans and projections, which requires another level of rigor and thought in growing your startup. That is when it is good. Many entrepreneurs crave that type of interaction, and many investors give it. But that is not always the case. That extra oversight can be limiting. Less experienced investors unintentionally can stifle good decision-making and make it difficult for the startup to make solid long-term decisions. No one intends to spoil or helicopter-parent their kids, but that does not prevent that practice from being commonplace. Unsure about that? Go to any local soccer field on Saturday and witness overanxious parents firsthand!

Bootstrapping allows the entrepreneur to control the startup's pace of growth.[16] Investors' motivations are influenced by their fund performance and timeline. That can have more to do with their overall fund performance and fund life. These drivers are not always in sync with what the startup needs.

Venture capital funds typically have a ten-year fund life. When venture capitalists pitch their LPs to invest in their fund, the expectation is that investing the capital and yielding returns from those investments will happen within those ten years. This expectation pressures the VCs to sell their investments after ten years—even if they perform well.

These things can have nothing to do with the startup's performance but influence how a venture capitalist views the startup. If successful, the startup will eventually receive acquisition offers. They may be good. They may be great.

They may not. But, as an entrepreneur, you may receive undue pressure to take one of these offers even if it makes less sense for you and your team in the long run.

The opposite may also be true. More investment comes with higher expectations. A $20 million sale of a bootstrapped startup could be life-changing for the entrepreneur. If the startup has raised multiple rounds of venture capital, that type of sale might be uninteresting to its investors. That is part of the deal with investors. Their priorities may be different from the entrepreneur's.

Loss of control correlates with loss of focus. It is important but time consuming to work with your investors. This comes at the expense of focusing less on customers and employees. The priorities can get mixed up in the entrepreneur's mind. Are investors or customers the focus? If the startup becomes dependent on outside capital and unwittingly loses focus on the customer, it can crumble quickly. In this case, the entrepreneur would have been better off avoiding investment, focusing on the startup's customers, and building a better business over time.

Bootstrapping lets you stay in control and keep your options open. Venture capital is rocket fuel for a startup, but it is fuel that can send the startup on an amazing trip to the moon or into the side of a nearby mountain. Best for the entrepreneur to take those tradeoffs into consideration.

IT VARIES

Every entrepreneurial journey is different. The Bronto story is *a* story, not *the* story. There are multiple ways to build a great startup. With that in mind, bootstrapping does not necessarily make sense for every startup. There is no moral high ground in bootstrapping a startup or, on the other hand, in raising round after round of venture capital. The answer is always: it varies. Being thoughtful and deliberate when building and financing your startup is important. If you do raise outside capital, raise deliberately!

Bronto could have raised venture capital along its journey. If it had, the company would have evolved differently—likely better in some ways and worse in others. I am happy with how Bronto evolved. Bootstrapping Bronto was the right way to go for several reasons:

- Focus. Investors can bring benefits beyond money, like mentorship and experience. But working with investors also requires time and focus—often at the expense of your customers and employees. Chaz and I could focus exclusively on our customers and employees by bootstrapping.
- Control. Chaz and I were particular about the company's culture and long-term growth. Every investor wants a startup to be successful in the long term. Still, the investors will never understand the business as well as the entrepreneur who is working in it every day. With bootstrapping, Chaz and I could control the quality of the entire experience—for our customers and employees—without outside distraction or interference. We preferred to build a startup that way.
- Financial. Chaz and I owned most of Bronto outside an option pool we had created for employees. When we finally did sell, not only did Chaz and I have a life-changing financial outcome for our families, but there were nice payouts for everyone in the company. If we had taken venture capital, maybe Bronto would have

been worth billions of dollars and been an industry behemoth. Or, maybe Bronto would have crashed and burned in the first few years. We chose a path which we believed had a higher chance of success and benefited from that.

Bootstrapping is not a binary idea. Startups go through long journeys and make different decisions at different points. A startup may begin by bootstrapping and raise venture capital later, or it may raise a round of venture capital early on but spend later years growing its cash flow.

The challenge is to be thoughtful and deliberate about how you finance the startup at each stage and be aware of the trade-offs—because money is never free and is usually the most expensive and most erroneous taken at the earliest stages. This dilemma is particularly true with venture capital and new entrepreneurs. They may inadvertently set their startup up to fail if they are unaware of the trade-offs. A better road is often to start bootstrapping without assuming venture capital is necessary to build a startup. This approach lets you work out the kinks in the business before poorly spending the most expensive capital you will likely ever get. This approach does not beckon cool headlines, but it is often better in the long run.

The Bootstrap Model differs from the Silicon Valley Model and its "go big or go home" approach. It is crucial to understand and be thoughtful about your startup and what you want before falling mindlessly into one model or another. Every entrepreneur's path is different, and the goal is to read the tea leaves and figure out which path is best for the startup and its founders.

THE BOOTSTRAP MINDSET

Launching and growing a startup takes time. Jumping into the unknown is scary and difficult. Pushing into uncertainty requires mental fortitude. Traveling the startup journey is much like running a marathon. Building Bronto was certainly a marathon for Chaz and me. Anyone who has run a marathon knows that physical preparation is only part of the battle. The mental fortitude required to train month after month and stay focused on running, instead of quitting, for three, four, or five hours is very difficult, even if you are fit.

Success in running a marathon relies heavily on the right mindset. Launching a startup, especially a bootstrapped one, is no different. Through my journey with Bronto and with what I have witnessed while mentoring other startup founders, I have found that successful founders often have the right mindset—a bootstrap mindset.

CONJOINED TRIANGLES

Silicon Valley is not just a place or a funding model—it is the title of a television show that aired on HBO between 2014 and 2019. *Silicon Valley* followed the trials and tribulations of Richard Hendricks and his motley crew of hackers as they founded Pied Piper and grew it into the hottest tech startup in Silicon Valley. The show plots did this while mocking the more ridiculous aspects of startup life.

In one episode, Richard is introduced to the "Conjoined Triangles of Success" by their newly hired professional CEO. The episode is hilarious and pokes fun at professional CEOs and their MBA degrees. Since life often imitates art, as a fan of the show and a connoisseur of business school frameworks, I present my version of a triangle framework, "The Conjoined Triangles for Bootstrap Success."

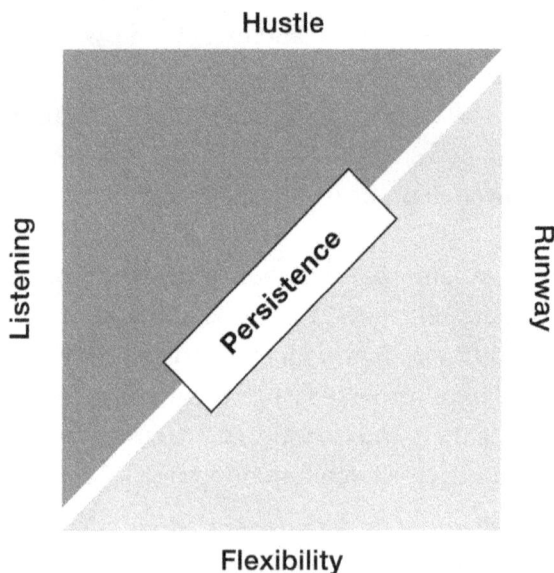

The Conjoined Triangles for Bootstrap Success

This framework describes the personal attributes I have seen to be helpful for a founder in starting a business—especially a bootstrapped one. These attributes make up the Bootstrap Mindset.

Let us dig into the parts.

HUSTLE

Starting and growing a high-growth startup, bootstrapped or not, is difficult. It sounds great—being independent, having potential fame and fortune, being your own boss, etc.—but the reality is often different. Ask any entrepreneur who is in the thick of it. She will be battle-worn!

One of the challenges in starting a business is getting momentum. How do you get moving? In larger, more mature organizations, the work comes to you, and you react to it. That can still be hard. But it is different when you work alone, and nothing is floating your way. All activity has to be self-created. That is why hustle is very important. You have to create your own activity. If you have this mindset, then you will do well.

In startup speak, hustle means getting out of your comfort zone. You can create a great product or deliver a great service, but if no one knows about it, then it will go nowhere. Hustle is about making a hundred cold calls to get to one yes—one yes to whatever you are selling. Hustle is about stirring up business. It is nerve-racking, even for experienced salespeople, to drum up business. Most people, especially those who have not been seasoned salespeople, do not enjoy the process, but successful entrepreneurs know its importance.

In the early days of Bronto, we did not have a marketing budget, and the world was not beating a path to our door. But Chaz and I had our brains, abilities, and, most importantly, hustle. Our early beta customers came from bartering our services with local media outlets. Then, we leveraged these experiences into getting paying customers. Early on, we knew we could not compete with our more established competitors. Their prices were better. Their product was more refined. But we could out-hustle them.

There is always room for a new competitor willing to work harder. Bronto was that young, scrappy competitor in the early days. Of the successful startup founders I have mentored and invested in, entrepreneurial hustle was always the most essential and important attribute I looked for.

LISTENING

Prajna is a Sanskrit word that means "transcendental wisdom or supreme knowledge in Buddhism gained through intuitive insight."[17] I have always liked this word, especially when thinking about startup founders. Startups are full of distractions and full of noise. This noise makes it difficult for entrepreneurs to understand what their customers want. Prajna speaks to transcending the noise to understand what is going on. In simpler speak, prajna translates into listening—really listening—to what your customers want. Great entrepreneurs do this and deliver what is needed to the market without being sidetracked by the noise.

The noise can be your desire to build something that you find interesting but is not wanted by customers. Or the noise can be spending too much time debating the colors of your business cards versus speaking with potential customers. It is easy to be busy. It is hard to be productive. The noise is alluring, like the siren's song of Greek mythology. Sirens drew ancient mariners from peaceful waters to crash into rocky shores. The noise can do the same for entrepreneurs and their startups.

Throughout my entrepreneurial journeys, sometimes I have had prajna, and sometimes I have not. I always failed when it was missing. DatabaseApp was a product I worked on for over a year after leaving my job at Red Hat and before starting Bronto. Although working on the product was helpful because I learned web development skills, the product went nowhere because I did not have prajna. I was so enamored with building the product that I was less interested in listening to prospective customers about what they wanted in the product. This was the problem that I had when building DatabaseApp. It is a very common problem with technical founders who like to build. Why? Builders love to build!

Things were tough at this stage. I had developed DatabaseApp for over a year with little to show. Karalyn and I were having a baby in six months, to add to the pressure. I had a sense of urgency in getting something off the ground. I rightfully believed that this post-Red Hat entrepreneurial excursion would come to a swift and brutal end unless I figured something out. This pressure brought me some prajna. This pressure helped me focus, strip away distractions, and force me to acutely listen to what would make a useful product.

I crafted BrontoMail out of DatabaseApp's ashes in a couple of weeks. Then, I spent more time visiting prospective customers. I listened first and then developed second. With this new approach, we were off to the races. Thanks, prajna!

FLEXIBILITY

In the summer of 1983, the movie *The Karate Kid* hit the big screens. As an energetic twelve-year-old, I walked a mile from my house to watch it with friends at the Fairlawn Plaza Theater in Akron, Ohio. The movie was a classic '80s flick. For those unfamiliar with the plot, the movie was about Daniel LaRusso, played by a young Ralph Macchio, who moves to a new town with his mom. Of course, older high school bullies, all part of the karate club Cobra Kai, immediately target and bully him until he is saved one day from a beat down by Mr. Miyagi, played by Pat Morita, neighborhood geezer and unlikely karate master. The inevitable training takes place. Daniel learns karate, defeats the bullies in the big karate tournament, and wins the affection of pretty cheerleader Allie, played by Elisabeth Shue. All is well in the world again. The good guys win. The bad guys lose. Down with Cobra Kai!

The central plot point of the movie is Mr. Miyagi training Daniel, or Danielsan, as Mr. Miyagi would say, on the basics of karate, except he does not train him explicitly. He makes him paint his fence, scrub his deck, and do household chores—but in a particular way. After days and days of doing these mundane tasks, Daniel complains that his supposed training was a simple ruse to do house projects for Mr. Miyagi. As a teenager, I sympathized with his apparent plight. As a parent, I have mad respect. As Mr. Miyagi soon reveals to Daniel, his specific requests, with precise hand movements, were training him in karate's core movements for striking and defending. "Wax on. Wax off." I loved that scene. Watch it if you can. It is a classic.[18]

The movie has a great entrepreneurial message. Sometimes, the least obvious experiences result in the most helpful benefits. This message applies to entrepreneurs as well as aspiring karate masters. Great entrepreneurs have skills that, at first glance, would seem irrelevant to starting a business. You should tap into those "Karate Kid" moments when starting a business. Tapping into earlier diverse experiences are especially important for bootstrapped entrepreneurs who have to rely more on their hustle and creativity to get things off the ground. They do not have the benefit of investor capital to fill in the gaps.

As a founder, you have to do a bit of everything. That is one of the big differences compared to working for someone else in a larger organization. Larger organizations have enough resources so everyone can specialize. These resources come with being big and successful. But things do not start that way. Startups are under-resourced. To start, the entrepreneur needs to be versatile and flexible. Can you code? Can you sell? Can you design? Can you recruit? You need to do a little of everything in the early days of a startup.

Juggling everything can be overwhelming. Unfortunately, startups are messy, but everything does not have to be perfect. Often, your talent as an entrepreneur is to string some ideas together to move them forward enough to turn them into something real. As Voltaire said, "Perfect is the enemy of good." This is certainly true for bootstrapped entrepreneurs.

When starting Bronto, I tapped into my early middle school experiences in hacking together a simple product. Also, I tapped into my Peace Corps experiences in operating in an unfamiliar and often uncomfortable environment. My teaching experience in the Seychelles and Ecuador helped me communicate with and motivate the Bronto team as it grew.

Those were the "Karate Kid" experiences that crafted me. I did not pursue them initially because I hoped they would help me as an entrepreneur down the road, but, in hindsight, they taught me invaluable skills and were critical to my entrepreneurial successes. Every entrepreneur gains these helpful powers, usually from the least expected experiences.

Flexibility is about being open to such tasks and welcoming them. It is also about pulling upon diverse experiences while wearing multiple hats.

RUNWAY

There is a classic entrepreneur adage that says startups always take twice as long and cost twice as much as expected to get going. Every startup journey inevitably has unpredictable twists and turns along the way. This was certainly the case for me and Bronto. While I left my job at Red Hat in the summer of 2000, I did not incorporate BrontoMail with Chaz until almost two years later. And Chaz and I did not pay ourselves a salary until a year after that. And that first paycheck was tiny. I did not expect it to take that long to earn income again. The Boy Scout's motto is "Be prepared." I was.

The preparation came in several forms. While in business school, I took a course in entrepreneurship. A retired West Coast venture capitalist was the guest speaker for one class. Within his talk, he passed on one of the simplest but most helpful bits of advice for my entrepreneurial journey—"keep your burn rate low." In other words, live cheaply and work cheaply. Fortunately, Karalyn and I were already wired this way.

Like all Peace Corps volunteers, I lived a modest life while serving overseas. This modest life continued while Karalyn and I were teachers in Ecuador and later living in North Carolina. While I was in business school, Karalyn worked at a job so we could survive on her salary. Even after I graduated, we kept our "burn rate low." This shared mentality helped us survive while I was without a salary for several years in Bronto's early years.

Change is hard. This is especially true when downgrading one's standard of living. It is easier to stay living modestly in the first place. Startups are challenging and can take a lot of time to get moving. A modest life gives one a longer runway to figure out the startup.

The second part of the preparation was savings. Karalyn and I were aggressive savers. We have always lived below our means and socked away the rest. In the early days, much of these savings went towards paying off my student loans. I deferred my undergraduate student loans for several years while in the Peace Corps and in graduate school. After deferring for six years, I had to pay them back. Fortunately, we had saved some money in the interim to do so.

Third, we made life choices based on our financial situation to give us more options in the future. For example, one of the reasons that I attended business school at the University of North Carolina versus other places was because I could attend as a newly in-state resident for a fraction of the cost of attending a private business school elsewhere. Debt matters. We made life choices to minimize it to extend my future entrepreneurial runway.

Finally, we had a bit of luck. Less than six months after I joined Red Hat, the company had its initial public offering (IPO). Nine months later, in March 2000, with the dot-com bubble bursting, Red Hat's newly minted shares crashed with those of most technology companies. Despite that, we netted out ahead with a little nest egg from selling those shares. This nest egg made it possible to quit my job and, combined with some good choices, extended my runway for starting Bronto.

RUNWAY AND RESOURCEFULNESS

Some entrepreneurs come from wealthy families, but most people do not. In my case, my extended runway was critical to my success. Bronto would not have happened with a shorter runway. This is often true for bootstrapped entrepreneurs who invest more of their own time to get going.

Extending one's runway relates to the other sides of the conjoined triangles. Hustle gets customers and users and maximizes the limited runway. Flexibility minimizes the "burn rate." It is expensive to hire others. It is usually cheaper (and faster) to do a "good enough" job yourself, at least to prove the initial concept. Some people call this being scrappy.

This was my experience with Bronto. I could not afford to hire a software developer to create the product. I needed to create a simple version of it myself to get started. So, my first task after leaving Red Hat was to learn how to develop software on the web. This was after working as a marketer for Red Hat and attending business school, where we learned about finance, operations, marketing, and other business topics. Nothing technical like coding software.

Learning to code was challenging to do by myself. The year was 2000, so online tutorials were not as prolific as they are now. Google was still new. This self-learning path was hard and time-consuming, but it was critical to Bronto getting off the ground. Was it the best use of my time? I do not know. But, when you have little, you do not have the luxury of asking, "what if?" You just move forward with what is in your control.

PERSISTENCE

Persistence is the element that "conjoins" the two triangles. Starting and growing a startup is extremely hard. But it can be amazingly rewarding for people wired a certain way—albeit still exhausting. It requires tremendous mental fortitude to keep going.

Let us use Bronto as an example. By the middle of 2005, Bronto made over $1 million annually. This was more than double the year before. This was three years after Chaz and I had incorporated BrontoMail and five years after I left my job at Red Hat to figure out the next great thing. Those were long years that required tremendous mental fortitude to keep going. It was not easy.

Chaz and I continued the Bronto journey for another ten years. Throughout the journey, we often joked that it felt like a knife was pressing against our throats—always threatening us to grow faster. It was not relaxing. Often, entrepreneurs will say that pressure comes from their investors. The best entrepreneurs put that pressure on themselves, whether they have investors or not. Successful entrepreneurs are very internally motived and have a strong sense of urgency.

The elements of the conjoined triangles are important for all entrepreneurs. This does not just apply to bootstrapped entrepreneurs. If a startup seeks investors, these attributes in the entrepreneur are the same as what any good early-stage investor is looking for. The best investors realize that investing in a startup is about investing in the founder and their commitment to go through "hell or high water" to move their startup forward.

Demonstrating that commitment through your preparation and previous experiences is essential—because you will need to pull on that background somewhere in your journey.

THE THREE GS

Great companies take time to build. Building Bronto was no different. From its founding to its eventual sale, Bronto might seem like one long story. It is not. It is three stories. As Bronto's co-founders and central characters, Chaz and I had to operate very differently in each story. This is true for all entrepreneurs who go through a similar journey. The roles change as you go along.

Well-trained MBA students worth their salt understand that any marketing or business strategy concept worth knowing must have a framework behind it. Bonus points are given if the concept's name comprises a number with a single letter. I am looking at you, three Cs (customer, competitors, and company) and three Ps (pricing, product, and packaging)!

To that end, I present the three Gs of the startup journey—Genesis, Growth, and Graduation. It comes with a nice visual depiction to double down on something good. I will take my PhD in startup strategy now. Thank you.

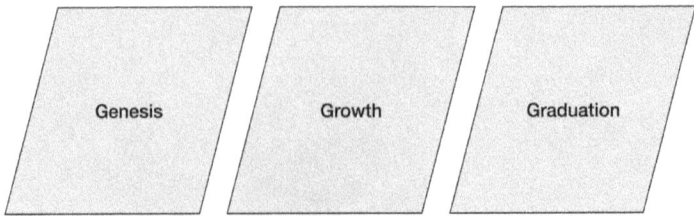

The three Gs of the startup journey

THE THREE STAGES

The Three-G framework describes the three stages of the startup journey. Each stage has a G-name for the sake of simplicity. What is not simple is that each stage requires an entrepreneur to think and act differently. The entrepreneur needs to play a different game at different stages. And each game requires a different approach, tactics, and leadership styles to be successful.

Through my startup journey, I have seen that the skills required to start a business are different from those needed to grow a business. Or, as I like to say more simply, "different games for different times." That is the spirit behind the Three-G framework.

Entrepreneurs, like most people, tend to repeat what has made them successful in the past. It is human nature. This strategy makes a lot of sense within a stage of the startup journey, but it is often the exact wrong approach for the subsequent stage. Entrepreneurs must play different games at different times or fall prey to the Entrepreneur's Paradox. The Entrepreneur's Paradox is that what you need to do to get started may be the opposite of what you need to do to grow or scale.

Let us dig into each stage and see how that applies.

GENESIS

The Genesis stage is about doing everything yourself. Individual heroics rule the day. It is the YOU stage. What can YOU do? What can YOU scrap together? Can YOU hustle your way to get customers? This is especially true for bootstrapped entrepreneurs who do not have the benefit of outside money to hire others to fill other skill sets. Often enough, these entrepreneurs must find a way to scrape together a "good enough" product to sell to customers.

This stage is particularly acute for bootstrapped entrepreneurs. It is hard to push forward when you have little. In the early days of a startup, it is easy to get distracted and run down rabbit holes. This challenge is counterintuitive since typically one associates limited resources with having too few possibilities to pursue. But the reality is exactly the opposite. Everything is possible. Successful entrepreneurs listen to their early users and customers and build something that their customers would find valuable. There is a reason the motto of Y Combinator, the famous startup accelerator, is "Build something that people want."

At Bronto, we had this guiding principle: "Indigestion is worse than starvation." This means that it is more dangerous for a startup, especially a bootstrapped one, to pursue too many things (often poorly) than to pursue fewer things and risk dying. This was our rallying cry to focus. It is easier to say than do, especially when debating between what would seem like a few tantalizing opportunities. In the Genesis stage, focus is extremely important. This is also the stage when the risk of no focus is highest. This is when the environment is the most ambiguous and the direction is the least clear.

Entrepreneurs need to reinvent themselves with each new stage to be successful and move their startups to the next stage.

I have seen entrepreneurs do an amazing job getting their startups to generate a million dollars in revenue annually, only then to see their growth stagnate. They struggle because they are still applying old methods to a new game. For example, great starters in the Genesis stage often struggle to scale their talents and delegate to others—necessary skills for later stages.

In the Genesis stage, Chaz and I hustled and relied heavily on "individual heroics" to get customers and develop Bronto. I was the chief (and only!) developer. I coded the product at night while Chaz and I sold it to customers during the day. If we did not do it, it did not get done. It was hard. The challenges of this stage required Chaz and me to perform these efforts to acquire customers. We believed anything that did not drive revenue, even if embarrassingly messy, was a distraction. There is nothing like survival to keep one focused!

In 2002, Bronto made $17,000 in revenue. That revenue was made by hustling together a motley bunch of customers, each paying a little under $2,000 per year. Getting customers was difficult to do on a shoestring budget, with an immature product, while juggling everything else. We continued these heroics such that Bronto earned $700,000 two years later and $1.5 million the year after that. This scramble was exhausting but necessary for us to be successful. Most successful entrepreneurs have a similar story of hustle from their startup's earlier years.

Along our journey, Chaz and I evolved our approach to continue growing. As Bronto grew, despite our selling, supporting, and coding talents, we could not be directly tied into all aspects of the business. It was too much. We had to change, or Bronto would have stayed a little startup—limited by our abilities to scale ourselves. We evolved, were successful, and entered the Growth stage.

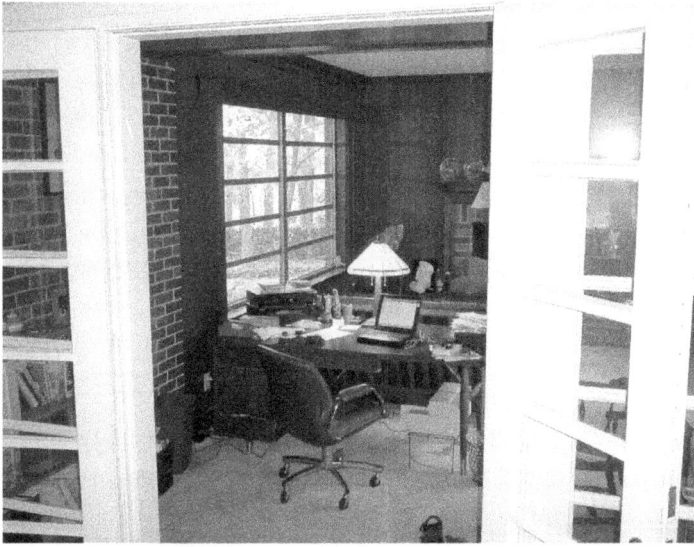

My home desk, where I coded DatabaseApp and the earliest versions of Bronto.

Me in late 2002, working in one of Bronto first offices, a windowless closet-sized room. It was within Regus, a shared office building in the Research Triangle Park area of Durham.

In the Growth stage, entrepreneurs add the executive hat to their founder hat. They must become the CEO (or COO or C-something)—not just in name but in practice. To be successful, entrepreneurs need to become strong managers and leaders—not the individual superheroes that led to their early success. They need to learn how to work with and through people to get things done.

Part of the transformation into an executive includes learning to manage teams, manage teams of teams, set vision and direction, and build operational engines that can operate and scale without their day-to-day presence. Individual heroics turn an idea into a moving startup. Once moving, the startup needs something different to become a larger entity.

This transition from honing the craft to managing others can be rocky. Most of us have had the unfortunate experience of being micromanaged. It is not fun. And it would not be fun for your team. This is a hard evolution for entrepreneurs because entrepreneurs are usually the best salespeople or developers of their products. No one is going to know the product better than they do. No one has more passion for it than they do. This strength is also the Achilles heel of the entrepreneur. To scale the business beyond oneself, the entrepreneur has to take a step back and enable a team. The entrepreneur may be better than the first individual salesperson or developer. Still, the entrepreneur will not collectively be as impactful as a team of ten salespeople or developers. The startup will never reach ten (or more) of these people if the entrepreneur micromanages them and fails to lead them well.

This evolution plays out in how the startup meets. Meetings sound terrible to many early-stage entrepreneurs. But entrepreneurs that are in the Growth stage realize how their teams organize around meetings is very important and evolves with time.

In Bronto's Genesis years, we had a handful of employees in the same small room. One would usually yell out their issue or question to get help. Everyone knew everything by startup osmosis—the act of being around. When we needed a more formal meeting, we spontaneously went to the nearby couches and talked through whatever the issue of the day was.

As Bronto grew, we realized that our original methods were no longer sustainable. The casual couch discussions evolved into a structured Monday morning meeting, on the same couches. As our team expanded, we ran out of couch space. This led to starting a Thursday lunchtime meeting with pizza—with everyone rolling their desk chairs to the space in the middle of the office. With further growth, we divided our meetings once more. We established a Monday morning management meeting for Bronto's de facto leaders and enhanced the all-hands Thursday lunch meeting. We upgraded from pizza to better food for our Thursday meeting and, over time, introduced numerous traditions to keep it fun and engaging for everyone.

The Monday morning management meeting became more formal, focusing on numbers, targets, and team initiatives. It was later limited to the Bronto Leadership Team—or BLT for short. With time, each functional team started their own meetings, and we also added a few cross-functional ones. Later, we added a multiple hour session every quarter to deep dive into every metric of the business. This was the Quarterly Business Review.

On the social front, our weekly team meeting moved to monthly and became more elaborate. Our couch-sized team grew to hundreds of employees so rolling our chairs together in the office was no longer realistic. We reframed it as a "Lunch and Learn," moved it to monthly, stepped up the food, and added a small auditorium to our office to host it. With time, we covered enough social and business topics during its time to augment it again. We added a Quarterly-All-Bronto, a half-day event for all Brontos. This was more simply known QAB. QABs were big events that included prepared presentations from all the functional leaders for the entire company to hear. Since we were international by this time, this included segments from our European and Australian leaders, too. It was a global event.

The point is that we changed. We had to rethink how we did things to communicate with the entire team. It became very important to keep everyone on the same page—so everyone knew when to zig and when to zag. Those needs were unfathomable and overkill when the team could still squeeze on a couch. But these changes were critical as we grew, and we would not have grown without them.

For the Growth stage, the entrepreneur also has to introduce a culture of measurability through metrics and establish processes to scale. The mentality shifts from hustle, hustle, hustle, hustle to repeatable, scalable, repeatable, scalable. The entrepreneur moves from working with a handful of talented superheroes and their individual heroics to leading an army of foot soldiers. The fuel moves from Red Bull to Microsoft Excel.

In the Genesis stage, Chaz and I could wrangle in another customer through our individual heroics. In the Growth stage, we had to be very organized about it. We had a rigorous annual and quarterly planning process that tied our sales goals to our sales quotas, attainment levels, recruiting requirements, and an alphabet soup of other important metrics to make our sales growth as predictable as possible. Running that type of operation required very different skills than the ones that got Bronto started.

Evolving into an executive is particularly challenging for younger entrepreneurs who have limited work experience and perspective on what it is like to work for others. Having worked random jobs earlier in my life did not help me start a business, but it did help me become a better manager and leader when I was running one. These "Karate Kid" experiences gave me empathy for others and helped me become a better leader.

Our efforts in the Growth stage paid off. Our quarterly sales targets soon exceeded our entire revenue from our first few years of existence. It was surreal but this is what happens when a startup grows.

The Bronto team in a larger office within Regus.

Eventually, we moved out of Regus to a small office on the newly developed American Tobacco Campus (ATC) in downtown Durham. This picture is of our team then.

Bronto continued to grow! This is our slightly larger team in our second ATC office.

GRADUATION

The last G stands for Graduation and is the startup's third and final step. Graduation is about the startup being acquired by a larger company and the entrepreneur transitioning from their day-to-day responsibilities and letting someone else guide the ship. Graduation is about architecting succession and continuity. At this stage, entrepreneurs need to execute their vision for exiting and then prepare to release control.

Bronto was acquired by NetSuite in 2015, but I started architecting a possible acquisition a few years earlier. This planning is essential for bootstrapped startups. The startup is likely immature compared to its venture-funded brethren regarding having strategic partners, thinking about valuation, and having the appropriate legal and financial rigor required by an acquirer. A venture-funded startup is also likely to have these elements installed by a board of directors that also provides a level of external accountability for the entrepreneur—ideally. When venture capitalists invest, these things are dealt with early in the startup's life.

Chaz and I now had to put on a different hat—an investor's hat—to prepare Bronto for this stage. We evolved from being scrappy entrepreneurs in the Genesis stage to being the executives of a high-growth startup in the Growth stage. The responsibilities shifted from the individual heroics of coding at night and selling during the day in the early years of Bronto. We had to, yet again, play a different game at a different time. As CEO, I had been heads down and focused on growing the startup for years. Now, I had to rethink my role and become seasoned in raising capital and pitching outside parties. That reinvention successfully led to the acquisition of Bronto.

After Bronto was acquired, Chaz and I stayed working at the combined company for a year to integrate the companies. This period required reinventing as well transforming what we had built for over fifteen years into operating as part of a larger company. Easier said than done! The secret is reinventing what kind of entrepreneur, executive, and investor one needs to be for the game they are in.

Like all things in life—knowing what should be done is one thing, but actually doing it is another. The transition requires self-awareness and the ability to change. As humans, we struggle with that. Bootstrapped entrepreneurs have to be scrappy to survive. If talented, their startup might get a few million dollars in revenue. But the startup will stay relatively small unless the entrepreneur evolves. Chaz and I did that at Bronto. This evolution is why we scaled a startup from nothing to over $40 million in annual revenue while staying top leaders until it was acquired many years later.

The most valuable aspect of the journey was that we got to experience each step. Because of the many years of building, refining, and evolving, we created something of value for our customers and, ultimately, for an acquirer. Many new entrepreneurs think that having an exit for their startup is luck. It is not. Building a valuable startup takes time and talent, and entering the Graduation step successfully, whether by acquisition or IPO, requires deliberate forethought and continual reinvention.

The evening before the official announcement, we signed the official documents and celebrated with the executive teams of Bronto and NetSuite. This photo shows, from left to right, me, Zach Nelson, the CEO of NetSuite, and Chaz Felix, my co-founder with Bronto.

THE MYTHS

There is endless advice on how to start a company. Read any business website. Listen to any startup guru (like me!). Scan any venture capitalist's social feeds. With too many sources, figuring out what is what is hard. Entrepreneurs can get demoralized when their path seems more challenging and less direct than those recounting their latest Silicon Valley success story. Fear not! You are not the problem. They are.

THE REASONS

Three things drive these disconnects. People have revisionist tendencies when telling stories. Ask your grandparents how they met. Chances are you will get a simpler, more romantic, more obvious story than whatever the reality was. Times were simpler then, as they say. As humans, we gloss over the details, especially the messy ones, and ultimately paint a more likable version. Our stories soften with time.

Successful entrepreneurs and business leaders have the same tendencies. Their startup's genesis story gets simplified and glorified with time. The media likes that. Better stories get more readers, and that is good for business.

The second disconnect has to do with the storyteller. Often, those doling out entrepreneurial advice have not been entrepreneurs. They played a minor role in whatever success they associated themselves with. Their role was more tangential to the driving entrepreneur of the startup. Or they joined it after the initial tough years when much of the ambiguity had been sorted out. This is the entrepreneur-by-association problem. This is particularly true when the startup was very successful. As they say, "Success has many fathers, but failure is an orphan."

The third disconnect relates to how universities have brought entrepreneurship into their curriculums. In the 1980s and 1990s, Wall Street was all the rage. Elite universities graduated flocks of students aspiring to be investment bankers and financial analysts. The best and brightest wanted the thrill and excitement of the industry showcased in movies like *Wall Street*, the 1987 film starring Michael Douglas, Charlie Sheen, and Daryl Hannah.

This adoration of Wall Street started to change in the 1990s. In 1992, the World Wide Web was born, and internet access was commonplace by the decade's end. Business school students looking for heroes shifted their attention away from Wall Street financial powerbrokers, instead looking to Silicon Valley hackers who could be crafting the next great thing in their suburban garages and college dorm rooms.

Business schools followed that trend and introduced courses on entrepreneurship. Most of these courses were designed from a business planning perspective, similar to how a course would teach an MBA student how to operate within a large corporation. The assumption was that the approach was the same, but the numbers would be smaller, and the issues would be fewer.

This was flawed. As we know now, the entrepreneurial toolkit for the Genesis stage is very different. No worries! I have come to the rescue with some uniquely entrepreneurial perspectives to dispel the common misconceptions about starting and building a startup.

THE GENIE IN A BOTTLE

One common myth is that startups pop out of ideas, like how a genie pops out of a bottle. The perfect idea is just floating around until some lucky entrepreneur thinks of it. Then she shares it with a high-profile venture capitalist who helps her raise millions of dollars, paving their mutual path to fame and fortune. Of course, that is an exaggerated spin on a commonly told storyline.

The reality is that ideas are cheap. Everyone has ideas. Ideas do not make great startups. Experienced investors and startup whisperers would rather bet on a great entrepreneur with a mediocre idea than a great idea with a mediocre entrepreneur. This is because everything starts as an idea—very briefly. That idea inevitably twists and turns when applied in the real world. Navigating that journey is the hard part of being an entrepreneur. And navigating that well is what makes a great entrepreneur.

In 2008, tech entrepreneur and author Eric Reis wrote a book titled *The Lean Startup*. The book "provides a scientific approach to creating and managing startups and get a desired product to customers' hands faster."[19] Reis's methodology centers around eliminating uncertainty by continuously testing business model hypotheses and using those insights to develop a minimum viable product (MVP), a prototype, to test the hypothesis with real users. Then, of course, iterate by doing it all again. This methodology is consistent with the keys to success for entrepreneurs bootstrapping their startup. It is what we practiced at Bronto before Reis coined the term MVP.

Remember "The Conjoined Triangles for Bootstrap Success?" Those critical elements of listening and persistence are what it takes to transform an idea into an MVP and beyond. With listening and persistence, the entrepreneur twists and turns the idea, planning the necessary ways to keep the startup alive and marching forward.

Unfortunately, aspiring entrepreneurs are often told a different narrative—dreaming up the perfect idea is an important and unique part of the entrepreneurial journey. Entrepreneurs spin their wheels, seeking funding for their startup just based on an idea and a good pitch instead of iteratively working on the problem and seeing where it goes.

This myth persists in the minds of aspiring entrepreneurs for a simple reason—it sounds good. This is why Hollywood continues churning out romantic comedies with the same old stale plot lines. They make for popular movies that are easily understood and widely accessible to a large audience. The message is that we all have a chance for a romantic comedy courtship, just like we all can dream up the next brilliant idea and become a billionaire. Good stories sell magazines, sell books, and build up your favorite tech billionaire's prestige (and ego). This keeps everyone incentivized to continue promoting the myth of the perfect idea.

First-time entrepreneurs are junkies for startup stories.

Seeking out the stories of others who have trod your path before you is human nature and healthy. This is why I wrote this book. Unfortunately, seasoned founders tend to revise and simplify their startup's Genesis story. Often, the simplified versions of the stories go something like this:

One day, while taking a shower or walking through a park, the entrepreneur gets an idea for a better widget. Despite having no track record or experience in the space, the entrepreneur pitches an investor on the idea. Boom. Presto. A multi-million-dollar investment happens, and a billion-dollar unicorn is born!

After the founder tells and retells the tale, their Genesis story is reduced into headlines, bullets, and soundbites, ready for the aspiring entrepreneur to consume.

When I started Bronto in the early 2000s, I did not have a unique solution. I was not trying to disrupt the email marketing industry. I had a solution to a problem. My friend Randy was looking for a better way to email his newsletter to his followers. He was using Microsoft Outlook. He had no idea if his recipients were opening or reading the messages, let alone if they were clicking on the links within them. The process was long and arduous. I jumped in and picked off his issues one by one. Then, I connected the dots to help his friend create and send his email newsletters, too. That was my starting point. From there, I relentlessly iterated on the solution for other people like them. After working with these early users, I had a legitimate product that I could charge money for, since it genuinely provided value and solved a customer problem.

The second challenge with the genie-in-the-bottle narrative is that "the idea" of your business will likely change. Almost every successful startup goes through at least one significant pivot before finding real success. Twitter was a marketplace for podcasts before it morphed into a micro-blogging platform.

This narrative holds true for more traditional businesses, too. William Wrigley, Jr. was a soap and baking powder salesman who started giving away free sticks of gum with purchases—until he realized the gum was more popular than his products! Today, Wrigley grosses billions and is one of the most recognizable brands in US history. He clearly was more successful dealing gum than middle-school me!

A SMALLER SLICE

In the late '90s, the dot-com boom raged, and interest in entrepreneurship flourished. At the time, I was studying for an MBA at the University of North Carolina at Chapel Hill. While there, I took a seminar on entrepreneurship, which consisted of the professor inviting various entrepreneurs and venture capitalists to speak about their trade. One of the speakers was an early-stage venture capitalist who argued in not-so-subtle terms that venture capitalists were essential to a startup's success. I remember taking issue with his claim and making a mental note, "Forget those venture capitalists!" I agree that venture capitalists can help scale startups, but he took more credit than was due and relied on many questionable assumptions.

He parroted one of the more popular assumptions at the time—the tech market is "winner-take-all." This means the leading provider in a category reaps most of its value. The logic followed that if the market was winner-take-all, it was essential to become your category's largest and most powerful provider. Second place did not matter.

In the 2006 movie classic *Talladega Nights: The Ballad of Ricky Bobby*, Will Farrell's character Ricky Bobby guided his life by his father's words: "If you ain't first, you're last!" That drove Ricky Bobby to become a NASCAR champion. That was also the mantra of the tech community and its investors in those years.

This furthered the narrative that venture capital was essential in fueling a startup to be as big as possible. The bigger, the better! The logic followed that this strategy would yield the best financial outcome for the entrepreneur. Even though the founder would own a smaller percentage, her end ownership and the financial return of the startup would be much greater in absolute terms—or so the story goes. This is the myth of the smaller slice.

This makes sense and works if the "winner-takes-all" assumption proves true. But that assumption often is not true. So, like with all important questions, the answer to whether a startup should take venture capital is, "It varies." As detailed in Chapter 2, entrepreneurs and venture capitalists can have different incentives. Venture capitalists make money from the size of the fund and the return on the capital invested. This requires them to invest a certain amount of capital, which can cause some misalignment with their startups.

Equity dilution is another factor that runs counter to the "smaller slice" myth. Dilution is the percentage of the startup the entrepreneur loses with each round of funding. Dilution is part of investing and taking capital is not inherently bad. Venture capitalists are not investing for charity! The important part, often overlooked, is that venture-backed startups typically have many rounds of funding.

The end ownership for the entrepreneur can be greatly

reduced with each funding round. As explained in Chapter 2, an entrepreneur is typically diluted by about 20 percent with each round of funding. That is fair since the entrepreneur receives capital to grow their startup. The challenge is when things do not grow as fast as expected. Simply growing may not be enough. The key is growing enough to counterbalance the effect of dilution. And growing becomes more challenging as the startup gets larger. Growing 100 percent per year is one thing when the startup is generating $1 million per year. When at $100 million in revenue per year, growing at a nice clip is extremely difficult.

Startups that do raise venture capital usually need multiple rounds of funding. With each round, the entrepreneur gets diluted. This dilution gets significant as time goes on. Many entrepreneurs calculate the odds and realize that bootstrapping and selling a smaller startup yields a better financial outcome for them. This is in addition to yielding other intangible benefits like the autonomy to craft the startup in their vision, without the extra responsibility of keeping investors happy and informed.

In one analysis, researchers looked at a database of 11,232 venture-backed startups that exited from 2009 to 2018 and found that 66 percent returned no meaningful capital for management. This period covered one of the longest bull markets in history with a hot mergers and acquisition environment and record amounts of capital raised and deployed by venture capital firms.[20]

That being said, many high-growth startups benefit immensely from venture capital. Venture capital can be great for fueling new products and opening new markets. The challenge is that this funding approach is widely over-applied to too many startups with business models that are not well suited for venture capital and the aforementioned Silicon Valley Model. In these cases, entrepreneurs would be much better off if they bootstrapped their business instead of raising venture capital.

BOOTSTRAPPED = LIFESTYLE BUSINESS

Another myth that annoys bootstrapped entrepreneurs is that their startups are lifestyle businesses. Oblivious venture capitalists sometimes imply this, and it is offensive to bootstrapped entrepreneurs because it conjures up images of working casually. It also implies that their startup is lesser than one anointed with venture capital. A lifestyle business is a company built by an entrepreneur that generates enough profit to let them work just enough to fund their lifestyle. The company is not being managed for, nor does it have the potential for, a significant return for an investor.

While there is nothing wrong with entrepreneurs seeking work-life balance, the implication is that bootstrapped businesses are second-rate or that the entrepreneurs are not trying hard enough. While this may be true of some small businesses specifically designed this way, it is certainly not true of all businesses that choose not to raise venture capital.

Bootstrapped startups follow a challenging path with many ups and downs. One of the benefits of bootstrapping the startup is that it gives the entrepreneur options in terms of how big the business should be. Some will opt to be small. Some will continue to grow big. This decision relates to the ambition of the entrepreneur and the nature of their business. Running a large business can be more financially enriching, but at a price of time and effort. Bootstrapped entrepreneurs have more control over that gauge. But they lose this control when they take outside investment into their startup.

Bootstrapped startups come in all shapes and sizes. Building a large, successful, high-growth bootstrapped startup in technology is possible. In Bronto's backyard is the SAS Institute, based in Cary, North Carolina. SAS is one of the world's largest privately held software providers. Founded in 1976, SAS generated over $3 billion in revenue in 2022 and was entirely bootstrapped by Jim Goodnight, its CEO, and its co-founders.

Another example is MailChimp. MailChimp was founded by Ben Chestnut and his co-founders in Atlanta. Like Bronto, MailChimp was in the email marketing space and entirely bootstrapped. Founded in 2001, MailChimp grew from its humble beginnings as a web design agency and organically scaled for twenty years until selling to Intuit for $12 billion. That is one of the most amazing bootstrapped stories in recent history.

WINDOW DRESSING

In the early days of Bronto, Chaz and I often reminded ourselves to focus on the window, not the window dressing. We defined the "window" as acquiring and serving customers, because everything else was a distraction or "window dressing." This mantra for focus is especially important for bootstrapped startups. When there is little time and money, everything not concerning customers is a distraction.

The trappings of "window dressing" tend to be the fun activities that first-time entrepreneurs concern themselves with when first starting. This includes getting an office, buying fancy furniture, designing the logo, ordering business cards, etc. These can be distractions. What makes a startup valuable is building and offering a product or service that others pay for. The entrepreneur should be able to draw a straight line between every dollar spent and selling more products. If the line cannot be drawn, the entrepreneur is focused on the wrong thing.

One source of this myth is confusion between correlation and causation. Correlation is when two things happen together—like peanut butter with jelly. Causation is when one thing causes another—like hard work and success. Startups are successful not because of fancy offices and slick business cards. They are successful because the entrepreneur built and sold something others want. Later, when the startup is successful, the startup invests in nice offices and slick business cards.

First-time entrepreneurs often confuse the correlation of these niceties with causation. Nice offices do not make successful startups. Startups become successful and then invest in nice offices. Entrepreneurs who see through this confusion can stay focused on their customers and hopefully help their startups be successful, too. They keep their eye on the prize and are in it for the long haul.

BETTER MOUSETRAP

American essayist Ralph Waldo Emerson once wrote, "If a man has good corn or wood, or boards, or pigs, to sell, or can make better chairs or knives, crucibles or church organs, than anybody else, you will find a broad hard-beaten road to his house, though it is in the woods." Sometime after he died in 1882, his quote was simplified to "Build a better mousetrap, and the world will beat a path to your door."

The reality for entrepreneurs is less kind. The world is not beating a path to your startup's door. The entrepreneur needs to go to the world and sell the product. The entrepreneur needs a lot of grit to get their startup growing. It is hard. It is not fun. Will Smith's famous quote in the 2006 movie *The Pursuit of Happyness* should motivate the entrepreneur: "Don't ever let someone tell you that you can't do something. Not even me. You got a dream, you gotta protect it. When people can't do something themselves, they're gonna tell you that you can't do it. You want something, go get it. Period."

Another hurdle when working on one's mousetrap is wanting the product to be perfectly polished before delivering it. This is incredibly challenging in the early days when the product is less developed. This is the story behind the famous quote from Voltaire, the eighteenth-century French philosopher: "Perfect is the enemy of good." In modern startup speak, Reid Hoffman, the founder of LinkedIn, reframes it by saying, "If you are not embarrassed by the first version of your product, you've launched too late."

This speaks to the importance of shipping ugly. The ship-ugly philosophy is sometimes summarized as "release often and iterate fast." The core idea is that it is preferable to launch a new product or new features of a product and iterate rather than hold back and "perfect" a product or feature before launch. Engineers, artists, and craftspeople often struggle with this the most. Their focus on perfectionism is awesome in most settings—except in entrepreneurship, where customer feedback gained from rapid iteration is paramount.

We hesitate to ship the products we build for several reasons. We are attached to the "ideal" vision of the product and convince ourselves we need to get across that finish line before sharing it with the world. We compare what we are building to the competition's product or think we must be the next Google before anyone takes our product seriously, forgetting that we are comparing our prototype to version ten of theirs. It is easy and fun to keep working on something to perfect it, but that is not what builds great startups.

This is where being an excellent developer or the best at your craft can be an albatross around your neck as an entrepreneur. You are great because you have high standards, and you should not give up those high standards, but you may need to shift your perspective. If you are holding back on shipping a product, all you can see are the risks to delivering now—the risk of putting out a software product with bugs. The risk to your reputation of others thinking you are not the best at your craft. There is a risk of disappointing your customers by not having all the features working as promised.

But you must remember there are risks to hesitating to ship your ugly product. First, you risk never starting. It is easy to put your idea on a pedestal. Before it is a reality, it sits there untouched, shiny, and you never have to face any problems. This is a comfortable place, but it should be a red flag telling you not to stay here long. It is important to get honest customer feedback as soon as possible. Otherwise, you fall into another trap: perfecting something that is wrong.

I fell into that trap with DatabaseApp. In my excitement about building something that seemed like the perfect solution, I never reconciled if it was useful. Bronto Software was born after I decided to scale back my ambitions and build something quickly based on solving a real customer problem.

If we hark back to Chapter 5, we remember to play different games at different times. Shipping an ugly or embarrassing product for a later-stage startup can be disastrous. But it is essential for early-stage startups. Until you have shipped your first product, you do not know what your customers will think, and you do not see the market potential until you have made some sales. So, start shipping ASAP.

Now that I dispelled these myths, your entrepreneurial toolkit is full. No—not quite. Let us discuss the importance of a startup's values.

THE STARTUP'S VALUES

Every startup has values and a personality that make it unique, often extensions of the founder's personality. As the startup grows and gains traction, great entrepreneurs want to ensure those values are not lost. As new priorities emerge and tasks come flying at you, your startup's unique personality might be dampened or drowned out. It is tough to keep track of it all.

Our parents teach us their values as they raise us and keep their fingers crossed that we do not completely abandon them as we become teenagers and young adults. The same dynamic applies to startups.

Chaz and I faced the challenge of maintaining our values as we grew Bronto. We wrote our values down as principles to help keep them front and center. Many years later, although we were many times bigger and stronger than in our early years, the principles rang just as true as they did in the early days. They helped guide our decisions throughout the Bronto journey.

These principles evolved organically as we grew Bronto.

We did not craft them in a vacuum. After a few years, we looked around, paid attention, and noted the beliefs that guided us, but were often unspoken. So, we scribbled them down. Doing so helped us remember our values as we grew larger, so that even the distraction of the day could not make us forget.

Continuously reiterating these principles helped orient new employees when we went through periods of rapid growth. In our later years, I printed the principles on eight pieces of paper and taped them up next to the engineering team to reinforce them with everyone. Even many years later, I find that once-Brontos still remember them.[21]

Every startup is different, and the entrepreneur will distill their startup's values uniquely. Generic values do not work. Authenticity is what matters. The values should be unique to the personality of the startup and the entrepreneur. That was certainly true for Bronto's values, which we dubbed as principles. We affectionately called them "The Bronto Eight."

Here they are:

PRINCIPLE ONE: CUSTOMERS DRIVE OUR BUSINESS

The first and arguably most important principle is "Customers drive our business. Success is guaranteed if we serve our customers. Customers pay our salaries, which is why we exist and grow as a company."

This principle may sound obvious. But when growing a startup, it can get lost. Over time, existing customers can be taken for granted, especially by new employees who don't know the customers' history with the startup. Companies do not have to exist. Companies must have revenue and customers.

Sometimes a bad vibe can creep in that customers are stupid and annoying because they have questions and issues. That mentality can be like a cancer that spreads throughout the organization. Sometimes, this cancer can be hard for entrepreneurs to see because they are distracted by the ever-growing obligations of running a high-growth company. With the entrepreneur likely no longer on the front lines, there is a natural and often necessary tendency to get abstracted from the customer and delegate the day-to-day interactions to teams of account managers, success executives, or similar roles.

This is a natural consequence of scaling. This principle was articulated at Bronto to counterbalance this sentiment. It kept the customer front and center.

PRINCIPLE TWO: HAPPY BRONTOS = HAPPY CUSTOMERS

The second principle is "Happy Brontos = Happy Customers. The best path to happy customers is through happy Brontos. We strive to provide a challenging, rewarding, and fun workplace. We understand that we can best serve our customers with enthusiasm and insight if we are happy and productive."

This focus on the employees (or "Brontos" in our case) was codified into our culture. At many companies, happiness can often be confused with perks—like having a foosball table in the lobby or a Friday beer gathering. But happiness is a lot more than that.

At Bronto, we did offer all kinds of perks, and outside observers would often credit those perks as the key to our great culture. But they were wrong. Our culture stemmed from our actions—the executives of the company, including me, listening to employees. Caring about their lives.

Promoting those who echoed our values and letting go of those who did not. Easier said than done! The actions of the entrepreneur and the leaders and employees who surround them are what matters.

One of the things I am most proud of is the culture we built at Bronto. Great companies are not born of great products or systems. Great companies are built and nurtured by great people. Many leaders want to know the secret to developing a great culture, and it is simple: Be human. Listen to your people. Spend time with them. Be transparent about what is happening within the startup. If you authentically do so, your team will make good decisions and work hard to make the startup better.

Culture stems from the top, or as is said, "The fish rots from the head down." The entrepreneurs—the leaders—forge the culture through their actions, how they operate and live their values, for better or for worse. The entrepreneur cannot outsource building a culture to another role or department. The leader sets the tone.

The extent of the entrepreneur's influence is particularly true for bootstrapped startups. Their startups tend to have fewer outside influences than venture-backed ones. The founders are often (hopefully benevolent!) dictators with high control over their startup and its culture.

Another unique aspect of bootstrapped startups is that they tend to hire more bottom-up versus top-down. Bottom-up hiring means that the entrepreneur starts with less expensive junior employees and hires more senior ones as the startup matures and can afford them. Of course, bottom-up hiring requires more leadership and management talent from the entrepreneur because junior employees are inexperienced and need more direction.

Venture-backed startups tend to hire top-down. They can afford to. To grow faster, the invested capital can be used to hire more senior people ahead of growth and the startup's revenue. The hope is that the startup will grow into the size of its payroll, and the increase in value will be worth the investment.

One can debate if top-down or bottom-up hiring is better. But remember that hiring affects culture. Less experienced employees, earlier in their careers, tend to be more impressionable and more likely to be molded by the company's existing culture. Senior employees bring a lot of experience and ways of doing things—some good, some not so good—which means they may not as easily adapt to the existing culture. Of course, there are exceptions. Overall, bootstrapped entrepreneurs need to focus on their culture even more than venture-backed entrepreneurs since their employees will most likely absorb whatever culture they are in. It is critical for their success.

We created several traditions at Bronto to make the culture engaging. For example, every month we hosted an all-hands lunch-and-learn. The sole purpose of these events was social connection. In addition to enjoying a meal together, Brontos looked forward to the "stupid human tricks" that all new hires were expected to perform. Any new employee would get up in front of everyone at the meeting to perform their own special quirky talent at their first lunch-and-learn. Another beloved tradition was community service. All employees were encouraged—and given paid time—to volunteer on service projects organized during the workday to connect employees further while doing good for our community.

These traditions made our employees feel as if they were

part of something bigger than themselves. And that feeling of a broader purpose sits at the core of building a great culture. Does an arcade machine or fancy coffee machine fit into the picture? Perhaps. But it is not the first thing that comes to mind. Bronto's traditions were an opportunity to reflect on the bigger purpose of their work outside of selling software, helping customers, or writing code.

Chaz and I lived Bronto's values in many ways. We did not have private offices, even when we had hundreds of employees. Also, we moved our seats to different locations throughout the company every quarter. We wanted to foster the values of openness and approachability, and our actions spoke louder than words in spreading the message.

PRINCIPLE THREE: INDIGESTION IS MORE DANGEROUS THAN STARVATION

The next principle is that "indigestion is more dangerous than starvation." We introduced this, as we reviewed the Genesis stage, in an earlier chapter. A rallying cry for focus, it is one of Bronto's most memorable and long-lasting principles. Focus sounds easy in practice, but it is one of the most challenging things for an entrepreneur to do.

In the Genesis stage, the entrepreneur often balances many challenges—the first is figuring out the startup. Who does it sell to? The startup is testing hypotheses in the quest for "product-market fit." Entrepreneurs try different things, talk to potential customers, and listen closely and carefully to what they say. They are trying to whittle down, read between the lines, and figure out what they should be selling and to whom. This is hard to do, and all entrepreneurs who figure that out become masters in the juggle.

Entrepreneurs must stay focused and not overextend themselves or their startups. They have limited time and money. It is tough. Startups cannot be good at everything. Even large companies cannot be good at everything. Focus is important. Entrepreneurs must spend their limited time and money on activities with the highest return.

In some ways, it can be easier to maintain focus in the early days of a startup, when resources are likely to be more limited. In the later years, with more success, it is easier to slip into hubris and think, "We are awesome. We can be great at everything." This is when this principle becomes most important. Staying focused is critical throughout the entire entrepreneurial journey.

PRINCIPLE FOUR: LIFT OUR COMMUNITY

The next principle is "Lift our Community. We are responsible for applying our passion and commitment to be a positive change in lifting our local community. We see this as an integral ingredient to being a stronger profitable company and stronger purposeful people."

Startups are tough. In the early days, survival is not a given, and usually, the scrappiest and toughest entrepreneurs are the ones who drag their startups to the next stage, come hell or high water! It can be all-encompassing. Because of that singular determination, other longer-term or otherwise "do-gooder" concerns can get lost in the dust. This includes supporting one's community.

Chaz and I, as co-founders, tried to lead Bronto altruistically. My personal beliefs about service to others were forged while in scouting as a teenager and as a Peace Corps volunteer after college. Through these "Karate Kid" experiences, I learned altruism has to be sustainable to have a long-term impact.

At Bronto, we supported the community while using our activities as a vehicle for recruiting and retaining great employees. We saw giving back to our community as an integral part of business. As part of that, we gave our employees two half-days per year to work together on community service projects with organizations like Habitat for Humanity.

Standing shoulder to shoulder building a house together, employees get to know one another pretty easily, developing relationships that spill into their lives outside of work. And yes, Chaz and I also rolled up our sleeves and stood shoulder to shoulder with everyone, hammering away. Working together on these projects connected us as a company and directly impacted Bronto's ability to move quickly and in the same direction as we strived to hit aggressive goals.

Encouraging your team members to do community service projects has other positive ripple effects. It attracts employees who value helping their community. And it opens a world of opportunities to those who have never experienced the joy of giving back.

I remember after completing one of these Bronto-sponsored projects, a new employee emailed me afterward to thank me for the opportunity. He said he had never done anything like this before and appreciated being exposed to a different way of being. He also said because of this experience, he would look for more opportunities to volunteer in his local community. This principle of lifting our community was extending beyond Bronto. Awesome!

PRINCIPLE FIVE: HITS, NOT HOME RUNS

One of my favorite principles is "Hits, not home runs." At first glance, this one does not seem very ambitious. But the rest of the text completes the picture. "Hits, not home runs. Consistent execution of our strategy day in and day out makes us a great company. Seeking the one big score and chasing fads, although appealing in the short term, ultimately does not help the company in the long term. Constantly striving for operational excellence is the key to our success."

When building a startup, it is tempting to swing for the fences and put too much faith in a magic bullet that will solve all your problems—if only Google would acquire us, if only a Fortune 100 customer would buy from us, etc. Dreaming is fun, but dreaming does not get the job done. Building a startup, like living one's life, has ups and downs. Sometimes it can be very hard. Startups, like the people behind them, are successful because they navigate the challenges of the journey.

This principle concentrates on day-to-day execution versus swinging recklessly for the fences. From the outside, building a high-growth business might seem like it takes unusual feats of strength. Realistically, building and scaling a high-growth business happens in the day-to-day, usually unexciting, execution. This is where growth lives.

PRINCIPLE SIX: MAKING SOMETHING EASY IS HARD

The sixth principle is "Developing intuitive products and services is difficult. The process requires endless iterations, relentless attention to detail, and the discipline only to include 'need to haves' and forgo 'nice to haves.'"

Startups take a lot of work. Entrepreneurs have to fight the gravity of the status quo and must build something better than the alternatives. Throughout the Bronto journey, we espoused simplicity in everything we did—at least, we tried. In the early days, simplicity was about creating an easy-to-use product. I always had a knack for that, so we will lump that trait under the founder's individual heroics. Having an easy-to-use product helped us get momentum in the early days. Later, we relentlessly focused on getting rid of "the crud"—old products, old processes, and old ways of doing things. I was quite dictatorial about it.

Startups naturally pick up crud with time. The crud may be minor and not a big deal at first. However, as crud accumulates, it can hinder growth. A startup can really suffer from it as time goes on. To keep growing, startups must constantly simplify.

Throughout Bronto, we had many versions of our product—Core Edition, Professional Edition, Agency Edition, and many more. As the years went on, we periodically re-formulated our product offerings and killed some legacy versions. In some cases, killing legacy versions meant losing customers. But, in the long term, the cost of maintaining old products outstripped the revenue from the customers using them. Having too many versions slowed us down, and we deeply believed that the opportunity in front of us was more promising than the opportunities behind us.

This crud in software development is referred to as technical debt. Technical debt is usually the result of less robust code written earlier in the products' history when a simpler solution would have sufficed. As the startup scales, code that is not robust will no longer be sufficient and will have to be rearchitected or rethought. Every software company has technical debt. It is the nature of developing a product over a long period. The challenge is to minimize the technical debt by constantly refactoring old parts of the code base. This is usually at the expense of developing new, hotly demanded features.

Crud is not limited to products. Sales organizations might have old quota plans. Customer service teams might be using antiquated tools for helping customers. Systems and methods that worked when there were a hundred customers might fail gloriously when there are thousands.

Crud is part of any startup. Constantly eliminating it is one of the keys to continuously growing.

PRINCIPLE SEVEN: IF YOU CAN'T MEASURE IT, DON'T DO IT

The seventh principle is "If you can't measure it, don't do it. Projects are rarely perfect out of the gate. They can always be improved. Measuring gives us the framework for that improvement and affords us the discipline to pursue only well-defined projects."

This principle sings a song that harmonizes with the other principles—focus, be deliberate, repeat what works, etc. In the Genesis stage, the entrepreneur needs to experiment and try things. If she can keep the burn rate low, she will have the space to do so. All the while, the entrepreneur has to be closely watching what works and what does not. The importance of measurement goes up as the startup scales beyond the entrepreneur's individual heroics. The principle of measuring—measuring everything—should be in a startup's DNA from the get-go.

Like the previous principle, measurement is not glamorous. Engaging stories that detail a startup's climb to the top rarely dig into the adventures of tweaking financial models or debating the returns on investments of various marketing spends. But that is the reality of startup building—despite its unappealing storytelling quality.

As a middle schooler, I was required to take a class in woodworking. One of the mantras of that class was "measure twice and cut once." You cannot uncut wood! Startups are not wood but are spenders of precious time and money. Be smart about it. Be analytical. Successful startups are deliberate about what they are doing and measure their projects. This lets them double down on what is working and cut what is not. Otherwise, the entrepreneur is cutting blind, and blind cutting leads to lost limbs!

PRINCIPLE EIGHT: PLAINSPOKEN WINS OVER JARGON

The eighth and last principle is "Plainspoken language wins over jargon and buzzwords. We pride ourselves on being clear, honest, and open with our customers. We don't hide behind buzzwords and business-speak. We believe plainspoken language is the most effective and powerful way to communicate with our customers."

Every industry has jargon—words and phrases that those deep within the space get comfortable with. Those things can be alienating and intimidating for others. It is hard to be open and authentic when one hides behind jargon. It is confusing for others to understand.

Bronto described itself as open and authentic. We expressed this in several ways. How do we write our job descriptions? How do we explain our product? I encouraged everyone to speak human!

All startups have value systems as they scale—officially or not. Whatever those specific values are, it is important to guide and nurture them. At Bronto, we were deliberate about recognizing and amplifying our values, and they were invaluable in shaping our culture and helping us grow rapidly.

Startup values matter. And startups with great values can grow to amazing heights, becoming very lucrative. This is when potential acquirers will come a-knockin'. This is when the entrepreneur needs to be prepared for the next stage—graduation.

THE BIG DEAL

Graduation is the final G in our Three-G framework and is just as important as the other stages. Many in the investor community would call this an exit. But, often enough, what qualifies as an exit for an investor is simply another stage for the startup—a graduation of sorts into the next stage of the journey.

Graduation can mean several things. The startup might be acquired, have an initial public offering, or receive a private equity investment to sell most of the business. This is Bronto's graduation story.

On April 23, 2015, Bronto publicly announced that Net-Suite would acquire it. The press release issued by NetSuite on that day said it all: "Cloud business software company NetSuite says it will pay $200 million to acquire Bronto Software, a marketing software company based in North Carolina. The deal is NetSuite's sixth acquisition and will be its largest yet."

NetSuite is a software company that provides cloud-based solutions for CFOs and others to manage their business' financials and operations. It was founded in 1998 and is based in San Mateo, California. Although NetSuite and Bronto were both cloud-based companies, our backgrounds and makeup were very different. For one, NetSuite was about fifteen times Bronto's size in terms of number of people and revenue. Also, their origin story could not be more different.

Bronto was founded by two young entrepreneurs with little money who built a business with several hundred employees and over a thousand customers in roughly thirteen years. NetSuite was founded in the 1990s and funded by Larry Ellison, the co-founder of Oracle and one of the world's richest people. He is worth over $100 billion today. Back then, Larry saw cloud applications as a growing opportunity, so he co-founded and funded NetSuite. This automatically gave NetSuite a tremendous leg up in the world of application software. Even after it went public in 2007, Larry and his family still owned more than half of the company.

Despite their different upbringings, on that day in April, Bronto's and NetSuite's paths came together. Bronto started a new journey, radically different from the one it had followed for the past thirteen years.

STRIKE ONE

There is a common saying in investment banking circles: "The best companies are bought, not sold." This means companies are acquired because they are great companies with happy paying customers, solid metrics, etc. They are not bought because they are aggressively promoting themselves to be sold. Like in life, the most desirable things are usually not the things being pushed on you.

But to be bought, you need to be prepared—not just structurally but also mentally. You have to be ready to sell your company. We were mentally ready for NetSuite, but only because we had gotten an offer several years earlier when we were not ready.

In 2008, we made a big change in our business strategy. We decided to narrow our target market from multiple industries down to just one: e-commerce. This change in strategy forged the beginning of our leadership in the new sector of commerce marketing automation. This would eventually lead to our acquisition by NetSuite.

By 2009, Bronto was bringing in about $5 million in annual revenue and had roughly fifty employees. In April of that year, our product team received an inbound inquiry from Salesforce. Salesforce was (and still is) the leading enterprise cloud-based software company. It was co-founded by Marc Benioff in 1999 and went public in 2004. Even in 2009, Salesforce was the largest and most innovative provider in the cloud-based software space. And somehow their product leaders found their way to our doors. But, to me, at the time, it was a distraction and made no sense. Bronto was focused on e-commerce, and they were not. Also, I had already planned a family beach vacation on Topsail Island, off the North Carolina coast, during the week they wanted to visit. I told my product team to relay that message. They were likely wise enough not to reiterate that exactly, but in the end, the Salesforce product team did not care and decided to visit anyway. I am thankful they overlooked my business naivete!

The visit went well in my absence, leading to more calls and more visits after my beach vacation. A few months later, Salesforce's head of corporate development called Chaz and me, and he presented us with an offer to acquire Bronto.[22] He presented an offer to acquire our company. His price was fair but could have been better. We balked, and the deal quickly fell apart. However, from that experience, we learned several things that helped us; we were ready when NetSuite became interested in us years later.

Even though we could not come to terms with Salesforce, we enjoyed getting to know their head of corporate development, and he provided us with some great advice. The most helpful part was that he noted we were not ready to sell. It was not that the company was not good—it was. It was not that we messed anything up—we had not. But we were not mentally ready to let go of building Bronto as an independent entity. He could tell that we loved what we were doing and were very committed to doing it our way for a while longer. That is a good way to determine if you are ready for the graduation stage. Ask yourself: Do you have action items on your startup's to-do list? Do you want to be the one to accomplish them?

The second thing that we learned from that experience was the power of having an intermediary. We negotiated the ill-fated acquisition with Salesforce by ourselves. We were not impartial. We were amateurs. We would have been better off using an investment banker or someone else to help us.[23] This was one of the disadvantages of having no outside investors or stakeholders in Bronto. Everything rolled up to me and Chaz, and we did not have a vested and experienced third party to help us. Related, we did not understand the acquisition process. Like most founders, we were newbies in this area. We learned from our mistakes and hopefully you will too. Be prepared. Be aware of strategic moments when you are in them. Plan accordingly.

The third thing that we learned is that not all acquisitions are the same. At the time, Salesforce had just exceeded $1 billion in revenue per year.[24] It was more than 200 times our size. With the differential, the Bronto team would have quickly been absorbed into Salesforce, and in short order, it would have devolved into just another product on the Salesforce price list. That could have been the holy grail for many startup founders, but Chaz and I wanted to keep the team intact. We thought of Bronto as more of an organization than a product. And overall, we were not ready to sell because we were still growing rapidly and profitably. We were having a great time and happy to continue building.

There is no need to rush graduation—all in good time and wait until you are ready. Graduations are more successful when it makes sense for the acquirer and the acquiree.

HELLO, NETSUITE

Bronto continued to march on. We surpassed $6 million in annual revenue by the end of 2009 and soon after rallied the company around a new mission. The new mission was to exceed $50 million in revenue by the end of 2015. That was five years away and ambitious for us to think about. We knew, to hit our goals, we would have to follow our own advice and play "different games for different times."

In the ensuing years, those different games included evolving my "fiercely independent" spirit and getting more comfortable partnering with other companies. My job as CEO, especially as we moved beyond one hundred employees and $10 million in annual revenue, was to think bigger and further out. This included expanding internationally to cover new markets, adding domestic offices to tackle enterprise customers, and partnering with our larger technology company brethren. This helped ensure that we continued to grow at a nice clip even as we dealt with the "law of large numbers."[25]

We expanded into Europe with an office in London (UK) in 2012 and into the Asia–Pacific with an office in Sydney (Australia) in 2014. To move up-market and bring on board larger customers, we realized that we would need to be geographically closer to them. So, in 2015, we opened small sales and service offices in New York and Los Angeles.

In 2013, we expanded our business development team to partner with larger e-commerce platform companies and actively work with them to create technical integrations and co-sell customers. We partnered with companies like Demandware (later acquired by Salesforce), Magento (later acquired by Adobe), SAP, and NetSuite. They ran the leading e-commerce platforms of the day, and were popular with our customers. Despite our humble homegrown roots, we became sophisticated with how to partner with others in our industry.

As my role changed, I spent more time spreading the word about Bronto in financial circles. If we had had outside investors, they would have helped to champion our company. Without investors, we had to do it all ourselves. I stayed plugged into the investment community by spending more time with investors and investment bankers. I kept them up to date with how well we were doing. I was laying the groundwork for something bigger down the road—whether it be an acquisition, large private equity investment, or an initial public offering (IPO).

My job as CEO—one of the many hats that an entrepreneur wears—was to help architect our future. Entrepreneurs must look for opportunities to set their business up for success and ensure that the future is bright.

By 2014, Chaz and I were getting tired and a little bored. Chaz and I had been working on Bronto for twelve long years. With four young kids at home, I was feeling increasingly stressed about the ballooning amount of time I needed to spend traveling to visit customers, partners, and our other offices. It was hard. But keeping in mind the old mantra, "The best companies are bought, not sold," I knew that building partner relationships might eventually lead to an acquisition or strategic partnership down the road. The Salesforce acquisition offer was an anomaly. Typically, startups are acquired by companies that they have known and are comfortable working with. This is exactly how the NetSuite acquisition came together.

As CEO, I could see the future in front of us would get harder. We would not be able to continue to grow revenue over 30 percent annually, year after year. We would have to do something—either raise capital to accelerate growth and set the stage for an initial public offering in a few years or be acquired. But, most importantly, Chaz and I were ready for something new to do. We saw the growth of a business as happening in cycles, and we did not want to reach a point when we were disinterested or jaded in leading Bronto. If we were going to sell, we should sell while we still enjoyed it. We should sell before we crested the hill in terms of our energy and excitement. And we felt we were approaching that crest in the hill. This is a good tip for all entrepreneurs— be self-aware of your own timeline. You do not want to "stay too long at the fair" as the saying goes.

In February 2014, as part of my outreach to the investment world, I planned to attend a technology investment banking conference in San Francisco. While there, I wanted to be productive with my time, so I reached out to meet some of our various partners, including NetSuite, which was in nearby San Mateo. That initial on-a-whim coffee meeting with NetSuite triggered a series of conversations and in-person meetings throughout 2014. The deal wheels had begun to churn!

WORKING THE DEAL

A deal entails selling some or all your startup and can range in complexity. Every investment round is a deal of sorts. In Bronto's case, we were selling the entire company. Since we were getting to be large, the deal was exhaustive and time-consuming.

The process took longer than anyone expected. Bronto was more prominent and complex in 2014 than we were in 2009 when SaleForce first approached us. We were a revenue machine on track for over $50 million and over 250 employees that year. And we were still growing at a nice clip.

To do things right, we hired a boutique investment bank to help us figure out what a possible acquisition might look like. Their team also helped us assemble a list of potential buyers and set up a series of "fireside chats." At some point, NetSuite expressed interest in taking a deeper look into our product and discussing synergies. These early conversations included Chaz, me, and a few internal product people to help explain the product.

Because we were on track to see record growth in 2014, the opportunity to sell came at just the right time, and we were ready. In 2014, our revenue was up 40 percent from the year before when we closed our books. So we were really busy—putting together the deal as well as actively growing the company.

In the fall of 2014, NetSuite sent us a Letter of Intent (LOI) and term sheet. This is the initial phase of a merger or acquisition. The company that wants to buy your company will send you an LOI and a term sheet with their offer. From there, we assembled a deal team, including attorneys and investment bankers. Part of what makes an acquisition so time-consuming is all the back and forth before signing a deal. It is common for deals to fall apart several times throughout the process.

We signed the term sheet at the end of 2014. Then, due diligence began. Investopedia defines and explains due diligence as "an investigation, audit, or review performed to confirm facts or details of a matter under consideration. In the financial world, due diligence requires an examination of financial records before entering into a proposed transaction with another party."[26]

Our head of finance, general counsel, and investment banker started gathering information and putting together lists of materials we needed to share with NetSuite. The paperwork at this point feels never-ending. As the CEO, when working on an acquisition, you can forget about doing much else, including sleeping. Still, you cannot afford to take your foot off the gas as you acquire and serve customers. The last thing you want is for the company to tank after you have come this far. So, this is my important piece of advice here: When you are selling your company, stay focused on execution.

There is a tendency to experience "deal-itis"—the fatigue that sets in from working too long and too hard on a deal. It is tough, but you have to keep pushing through. A common expression in sales is "Time kills all deals." This especially applies to acquisitions, since they are always more complex deals. It is important to keep the momentum because working through a transaction is exhausting on both sides.

This exhaustion is like the feeling you get when redoing your kitchen, which I have painfully done. The end goal makes sense and is good, but the process can be so brutal that you might regret all the choices you made during the transformation. Pro tip: Just move. ;-)

Also, working on a deal is highly distracting. It was essential to keep Bronto focused on growing the business rather than taking our foot off the gas. No acquirer wants to purchase a stalled business. We needed to keep our eye on the ball and finish strong.

We kicked off due diligence from a people standpoint in January 2015. We met with NetSuite leadership to start looking at the synergies between Bronto and NetSuite. We also started plotting about what Bronto would look like folded into NetSuite. Ultimately, we agreed that Bronto would operate as a separate entity under NetSuite's umbrella for the first few years.

Often, acquired companies are not operated as separate entities. It is very common for an acquirer to retain just the startup's product and its software engineers and lay off the rest of the company. That was not the case with Bronto, which is one of the reasons why we decided to work with NetSuite.

THE CLOSING

We announced the acquisition after the market closed on April 23, 2015. Since NetSuite was a publicly traded company, there were more hoops to jump through than if we had been acquired by a private company.

The night before, we finalized the paperwork and had a formal signing at 21C, a nice boutique hotel in downtown Durham. Then on the morning of the 23rd, we gathered the Brontos together for one last photo as an independent company in the courtyard of our Durham offices on the American Tobacco Campus.

Although we announced the acquisition in April, it was a few more months until the transaction was completely finalized. This is not uncommon. Working through the legal and financial aspects of acquiring a business takes time, especially when there are multiple international operations. However, there were some unique aspects that made the closing take an unusually long time.

There is always the possibility of an unexpected road-block when you are trying to close the deal. At Bronto, we were deeply interwoven with Salesforce for selling and servicing our product. It is an integral part of how we sold and serviced everything. Coincidently, Salesforce and NetSuite had a long-standing "frenemy" relationship going back to their genesis in the 1990s.

Salesforce and NetSuite had grown to hate each other, becoming fierce competitors, and were not above petty actions to foil each other. It was possible that once the acquisition was complete, Salesforce might cut Bronto from its systems. Salesforce would legally be able to because of some small print in their terms of service. Because of this risk, we needed time to migrate our systems away from Salesforce, and pushing out the closing date helped do that. Ultimately, no pettiness arose, but we were smart to give ourselves extra time to migrate our internal systems from

Salesforce, just in case. Always prepare a detour route for any possible roadblock.

On June 8, 2015, the acquisition closed and became official. Bronto was part of NetSuite. We received $200 million—half in cash and half in NetSuite stock. Everyone in the company received some form of payout in three ways:

The first was in the form of redeemed stock options in Bronto. We did not offer stock options for the first years of Bronto's life. We wanted everyone to focus on the business's long-term success and not consider it a transaction. This would be blasphemy for most venture-backed companies, but we found that investing in the culture and other benefits to enhance the employee experience was a better driver of growth.

This is not uncommon in bootstrapped businesses. Many in the technology space would take issue with this approach, but few can speak to it from experience. That said, we did introduce stock options in 2010 as we approached $10 million in annual revenue and one hundred employees. At this size, we needed to recruit leadership that had "been there and done that," and not offering options was starting to become a problem. So, we changed. We played a "different game for a different time."

The second was with Restricted Stock Units (RSUs). RSUs are like stock options except that they are actual shares of stock that vest over time, whereas stock options give the holder the option to buy shares at a predetermined price. RSUs can have tax benefits for the company and the recipient, so they are sometimes used. In addition to the $200 million purchase price, NetSuite granted $25 million in RSUs ($15 million at close and $10 million a year later) to some members of the team as a retention bonus.

The third was a $6 million fund which Chaz and I created from our holdings. Inevitably, when you build a company and put together initial offers for new employees, what you think a person will contribute, and what they actually contribute are two different things.

When starting at Bronto, some people negotiated great initial offers but were average performers. On the other hand, some Brontos joined early in their careers and stayed a long time. They often started with modest offers and turned into all-stars later.

This fund was the way for Chaz and me to address the discrepancies we sometimes found when an all-star's modest compensation or other acquisition-related payouts did not accurately reflect their significant contributions to Bronto's success.

One of the advantages of being a bootstrapped entity was that we had the latitude to make those kinds of decisions. It would have been more challenging if we had had to negotiate the $6 million fund with outside investors who were less involved with our day-to-day operations.

This is something to consider as you build out your startup.

THE LAST HURRAH

The tough part of any acquisition is integrating the acquired company into the acquiring one. Another unfortunate truism in the mergers and acquisitions game is that most acquisitions fail. They fail in the integration phase—often, those doing the deal underestimate the challenges in integrating one company culture into another one. Chaz and I suspected cultural integration was going to be the toughest part of joining NetSuite. And it was. But Chaz and I were committed to making the integration as successful as possible.

During one of our earliest meetings with NetSuite, Chaz asked NetSuite's CEO, Zach Nelson, "Why are you buying us?" His somewhat tongue-in-cheek response was, "You're smart people; you're going to help us figure that out." Ultimately, we did.

We developed plans to weave Bronto into NetSuite's company and culture. Chaz and I stayed at the company for a full year until the following April. We did not have any extra financial incentive to do so, but we had built Bronto over so many years and wanted it to be successful within NetSuite. We felt that our oversight during this fragile transition was critical to making that happen, and it was.

Integration is challenging for most startups. As an entrepreneur, especially as a bootstrapped entrepreneur, it is difficult to adjust into the corporate machinery of a larger publicly traded company. It is a different gig and requires a different game. Unlike our previous game changes, this time, Chaz and I thought it was time to start to begin our post-Bronto life.

Every startup celebrates its major milestones in different ways. This is how we celebrated our graduation. Our last day was April 8, 2016—a year after the announcement. Of course, in typical Bronto fashion, we had a big send-off replete with in-person and video goodbyes from employees that had come and gone over the last fourteen years, as well as a quirky bit of being led out of the building in handcuffs, being loaded onto an old pickup truck filled with hay and baby goats. We were officially "put out to pasture." It was a very Bronto-appropriate ending to that entrepreneurial journey.

THE MOTHERSHIP

After we left, Chaz and I stepped back into our personal lives and re-learned how not to be busy running a high-growth startup. Bronto continued to find its way, quarter after quarter, into NetSuite while still maintaining a fair amount of independence. Things were more or less the same after the acquisition, until they were not. This time, NetSuite was to be acquired.

NetSuite was founded in 1998 by Evan Goldberg, a former protégé at Oracle. The business was initially seeded with $125 million by Larry Ellison, the co-founder and CEO of Oracle. Over the years, NetSuite brought in other investors and had an initial public offering in 2009. As mentioned earlier, since Larry Ellison and his family owned almost half of the company, Oracle's acquisition of NetSuite was always a question of not "if" but "when." "When" came a few months after Chaz and I bid farewell to Bronto.

On July 28, 2016, Oracle announced it had offered to purchase NetSuite for $9.3 billion. After the offer was announced, there was a predictable scuffle between Oracle and its major investors because of the obvious conflicts of interest—Oracle buying a company at a premium in which their CEO has a significant stake. Nevertheless, the scuffle was worked out, and NetSuite and Bronto eventually joined Oracle. Oracle had almost 1,000 times the revenue of Bronto. Bronto had fewer than 300 employees. Oracle had 136,000.

Oracle did not intentionally acquire Bronto. It acquired NetSuite, and Bronto was along for the ride. Bronto's revenue and team were a rounding error to Oracle. Unfortunately, rounding errors are often forgotten and lost—which is what happened with Bronto. There is another tech industry quip: "Oracle is where good companies go to die." That is not always true, but it was true for Bronto.

Since the acquisition by Oracle, Bronto has slowly been assimilated into the larger entity. Most employees have expanded or shifted their focus away from selling, supporting, and developing the Bronto product, as the priorities have changed to be more consistent with Oracle's goals.

The final nail in the coffin for Bronto came in March 2021 when Oracle sent an email stating: "This notice is to inform your company that the Bronto Marketing Platform has been assigned end-of-life status, and the last date of service will be May 31, 2022." True to their word, on May 31, 2022, the Bronto product was shut off, and the idea that was dreamt up in January 2002 ended.

It was sad, but it did not come as a surprise. Many acquired companies go this route. Initially, the software stays the same, then changes are made, and more changes are made. Eventually, the product is integrated into the company's other offerings or becomes obsolete due to other emerging technologies or areas of investment. As an entrepreneur, you must know this will likely happen when you sell your startup.

Keep in mind that startups are not just products—they are also people. Some of them will become entrepreneurs and start their own startups and take leadership positions at other companies. When they do, they will bring a little bit of the company you created with them. This is what happened with Bronto; so, in that sense, the spirit of Bronto lives on.

So, even if the spirit of your startup lives on elsewhere, you have graduated from this entrepreneurial journey. Now, like any graduate, you have to ask yourself, "What do I do now?"

THE ROAD AFTER

Entrepreneurs often struggle to find a new purpose after selling their business. This is especially true for bootstrapped entrepreneurs, who, more often than not, have taken longer to build their startup. This was certainly true for me. Fortunately for me, I eventually found a few things to focus on after leaving Bronto in April 2016. Fortunately for you, these things are related to entrepreneurship and can help you on your journey.

One common piece of advice given to graduated founders, especially if they became financially independent, is, "Do not do anything right away." It is important to regain your perspective on what is important, and it is hard to sort that out if you are starting another new venture right after finishing a long entrepreneurial journey. After selling, I reached out to other graduated entrepreneurs for their advice about what to do next. They told me to wait a year before deciding. I could not. I graded myself with a B for waiting for almost nine months before starting something else.

THE COLOPY KEIRETSU

In January 2017, I started Colopy Ventures as a technology startup-focused family office. A family office is a privately held company that manages wealth for a family by investing in various public and private ventures. In my case, Colopy Ventures also acted as an umbrella to experiment with, invest in, and try different business ventures. The primary mission was to support and invest in technology entrepreneurs in the Raleigh–Durham area of North Carolina. I am a fan of proximity and like contributing to entities that are geographically closest to me.

I have tried many things during and after my Bronto journey—many failed—but I learned lessons along the way. And I wanted to share these hard-learned lessons with others. One of the simplest lessons that I learned is that entrepreneurship is always hard. Raising money early makes it more challenging. It insulates you from seeing the problems. Entrepreneurship is about solving problems. Great businesses are born through offering a product or service that people want and need. To sort that out, you need to be a great listener—one of the aspects of the Bootstrap Mindset discussed in Chapter 4. Money (and ego!) make listening that much more challenging to do.

The vision for creating Colopy Ventures was to create a *keiretsu* for startups—dubbed the "Colopy Keiretsu." Keiretsu is a Japanese term that refers to "a business network of different companies, including manufacturers, supply chain partners, distributors, and occasionally financiers. They work together, have close relationships, and sometimes take small equity stakes in each other, all the while remaining operationally independent."[27] The "Colopy Keiretsu" is a series of related ventures oriented around serving and supporting regional software entrepreneurs. GrepBeat, Jurassic Capital, and Primordial Ventures are the three entities that make up my keiretsu today and each serve software entrepreneurs differently.

GREPBEAT

GrepBeat is the center of the keiretsu. GrepBeat, as described on its website, is a "mission-based media organization whose purpose is to lift the tech community in the Triangle (or Raleigh–Durham to you outsiders). GrepBeat does this by telling the stories of this area's mighty tech startups and their entrepreneurs in an engaging and colorful way. Through a newsletter, podcasts, videos, events, and other clever things that we can dream up, we help today's small startups become tomorrow's industry behemoths."[28]

GrepBeat started in July 2018 when Pete McEntegart joined as Managing Editor. Shortly after, we launched a twice-a-week email newsletter summarizing the week's local startup news. Soon after, we expanded with a team of student reporters from the journalism school at the University of North Carolina at Chapel Hill. We now employ a small team of full-time reporters and digital producers.

My reason for starting GrepBeat was partially driven by my experiences as a struggling bootstrapped entrepreneur almost twenty years ago. When you are in the early days of a startup, you are not a success or failure. You are simply not seen, which is extremely demoralizing, slogging along day after day, building your startup.

GrepBeat has several purposes. First, GrepBeat aims to acknowledge the entrepreneur's journey by giving them early validation through media. Hopefully, that early exposure will help them grow in unpredictable and less obvious ways. The coverage can help find an early employee, intrigue a prospective angel investor, or help them acquire early customers. In all cases, a story validates the startup in the eyes of others and benefits in many ways.

The second purpose of GrepBeat is to help the economic development of the region. The Raleigh–Durham area is a wonderful part of the country but not a media center. Regions like New York, Los Angeles, and San Francisco have a disproportionate number of stories told about the startup successes on a national stage because these regions are also media centers. GrepBeat helps offset that.

The third purpose of GrepBeat is to create a sense of startup density for the area. Regions are successful because they have a density of similar companies. Some examples include the financial district in Manhattan, the venture capital cluster of Sand Hill Road in Silicon Valley, or Broadway's theater scene. GrepBeat creates virtual density through storytelling and "overcovering" the happenings of the region's startups.

GrepBeat has been rewarding and enjoyable for me to contribute to the community. For several years we hosted a weekly online show called *The Friday Nooner*. Every week, we interviewed a local startup leader and bantered about whatever was topical in the news and our lives. It was fun.

During the banter, I injected "real talk" and provided advice on the challenges and tricks of building a great startup. Entrepreneurs have to sift through a lot of noise. This can come from advisors who have never built a business. Even venture-backed entrepreneurs often have limited experience in building a business, because they artificially accelerated their business. As I've said, doing so can be great, but it also can mean that the entrepreneur risks missing out on learning some hard and insightful lessons in building a great business.

Finally, GrepBeat is also a strategic part of Colopy Ventures. As a local thought leader and news generator, GrepBeat keeps me and my other entities, like Jurassic Capital and Primordial Ventures, in the middle of the conversation about everything happening in the regional startup community.

JURASSIC CAPITAL

Jurassic Capital is a growth equity firm that invests in bootstrapped and lightly capitalized business-to-business ("B2B") software startups generating between $1 million and $5 million in annual revenue. I started Jurassic Capital in late 2019 with Kevin Mosley. Kevin worked with me at Bronto years earlier.

At Jurassic, we aim to fill an investment gap between early-stage venture capital and later-stage growth equity. We help startups through investment and hands-on expertise, so that they can continue to grow. We help them jump over the chasm where the "individual heroics" of the founders no longer are enough to fuel growth. Working through other leaders and teams as well as developing longer-term executional plans are necessary. That is where Jurassic specializes.

Jurassic's name relates to my affinity for prehistoric history. Jurassic looks to invest in startups that are similar to Bronto Software. Where do you go looking for a Brontosaurus? It is not a "where" but a "when"—the Jurassic Period. Jurassic was the geologic period between roughly 200 and

150 million years ago. Then, Pangea, early Earth's super-continent, started to break apart. Early birds appeared. The weather got warmer. And most importantly, Brontosauruses roamed the earth. These times were good. In addition to the prehistoric connection, the name Jurassic Capital shares my initials—JC.

Becoming an investor may seem ironic after having had a long career bootstrapping a startup and now singing the praises of bootstrapping in this book. But there is no one path to creating a great company. In Chapter 3, I discussed thinking through your business model when assessing the potential to bootstrap the startup or the viability of an influx of venture capital. The reality is that best answer will vary. And the mantra behind this book is that there is more than one way to build a great company.

Startups come in different shapes and sizes and ideally, their investment models and their providers should match as well. Sadly, that is not always the case. Too often, venture capitalists find it easier to follow the well-beaten path of what a fundable startup should look like than to try a new path with fresh eyes. This leads to poor investment decisions and a poor partner for the startup.

But some investors have had significant experience starting and scaling software companies. They share advice and wisdom at the appropriate times. They are well-positioned to help prepare the entrepreneur for the next level of growth because they have seen the patterns before, and understand the challenges and juggling that entrepreneurs face.

While building Bronto, I knew entrepreneurs who had bootstrapped their startups to $1 million in annual revenue—the same place Bronto was after a few years. Yet their growth stalled and flattened out, unlike Bronto's. Why? Was it the market? No—we were in the same market. Was it their funding? No—Bronto had no funding. Time and time again, the answer involved the execution. Often enough, the entrepreneur could create and sell a good product but then had challenges scaling beyond a small team.

When startups get initial momentum, it is typically because of the entrepreneur's dynamism and "individual heroics." But that strategy only works for so long. If one is successful at that stage, the "swoop in with my superpowers and move a mountain to launch a feature or land a client" approach does not get the job done anymore. There are not enough hours in the day. The entrepreneur and the startup must reinvent themselves. Simply said, they have to "play different games at different times." Scaling past $1 million in annual revenue is a different time.

Many entrepreneurs need help with this transition. The better ones know that their growth will stagnate unless they try something different. Jurassic aims to provide just that—something different. Entrepreneurs who are looking for investors should be looking for more than just capital. The right investors should bring their experiences, connections, and wisdom to the table too.

THE PLAYBOOK

At Jurassic, we see a common set of challenges for the start-ups that we invest in. These startups are beyond the "I have an idea" stage but are still small. To codify our efforts to help them address the common challenges, we developed a playbook.

Sales	Churn
Metrics	Leadership
Culture	Help

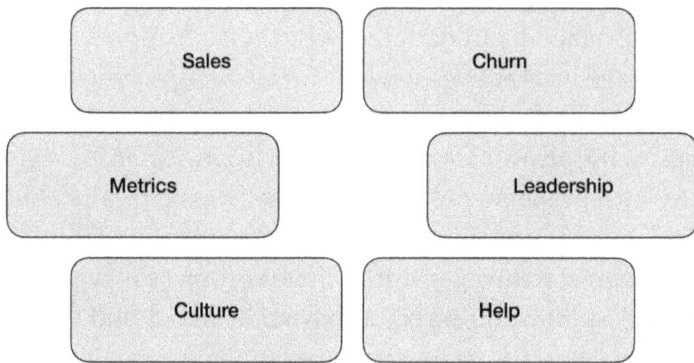

Jurassic Playbook for Growth

The Jurassic Playbook for Growth helps companies scale in a disciplined way, typically focusing on a few critical dimensions. The first is leadership. We have found that many startups reach a ceiling where the "individual heroics" of the lead entrepreneur no longer suffice to drive growth. Some entrepreneurs need mentoring and to learn to hire and delegate; others must be replaced. In either case, the startup needs help filling out their leadership team around the entrepreneur.

The second dimension is culture. Building a strong culture around a shared vision for the startup is important in achieving sustained growth. Bronto had a strong culture, and it was a big reason for its success. Sowing the seeds of a strong culture begins early and pays more and more dividends as the startup grows. Well-known business academic Peter Drucker said, "Culture eats strategy for breakfast." I have indeed found this to be true with all growing companies.

The third dimension is sales. Few early-stage startups have a sales process led by a strong and experienced leader. It is not surprising why, especially for bootstrapped ones. Experienced sales leaders are expensive and require a significant investment in sales and marketing to take advantage of their skillset. It is akin to buying an expensive Porsche but only for driving back and forth to the nearby local grocery store. It is what we call "overkill"!

Another dimension is support and churn. High-quality customer support is of paramount importance in customer retention and market credibility with all startups—especially for SaaS startups that rely on recurring revenue streams. To get beyond the entrepreneur's individual heroics, the startup needs processes and people to build the appropriate customer support, account management, and customer success teams. Otherwise, the risk of losing existing customers, also known as churn, increases as things fall through the cracks. Churn can easily offset and sometimes exceed the revenue from new customers. It is hard to fill a leaky bucket!

Next up is metrics. Startup growth beyond the early stages becomes more of a science. It requires rigor around measurement and reporting, especially in sales and marketing. This might be overkill when an entrepreneur and their startup are developing a product and fishing for early customers. Later, however, entrepreneurs need to develop a culture around metrics and reporting. This kind of culture can be very foreign to the all-hustle, all-the-time approach that got the startup through its first stages of growth.

The last piece is outside help. Successful entrepreneurs are scrappy. Chapter 4 detailed how attributes like hustle and flexibility are essential to get a bootstrapped startup off the ground. Things change when the startup achieves a little size. There is a risk of being "penny wise and pound foolish." Outside investors can help rethink the old ways of doing things and revisit where and how it is best to invest more capital in the startup.

With growth, more financing opportunities also become available. Getting investment for an idea, hope, and dream is very different from getting an investment for fueling growth with a clear calculus of how one dollar of investment can create two dollars in revenue.

Jurassic helps companies identify the gaps that startups might have in these areas and fill in where appropriate. For example, we might help recruit senior leadership to work with the entrepreneur and their team to rethink how they run their business. Often, it is easier for an outside party, like Jurassic, who is familiar with bootstrapped companies, to see what is working and what is not and guide the team for the appropriate changes. Founders are often so close to the day-to-day operations of their startup that it is easy to lose sight of the forest from the trees.

Addressing all these challenges is a tall order, which is why we created Jurassic Capital—to fill the gaps in the investment market as operating-centric investors.

PRIMORDIAL VENTURES

The third and newest part of Colopy Ventures is Primordial Ventures, an early-stage venture capital firm. Like Bronto Software and Jurassic Capital, the name was inspired by a prehistoric scientific theory—"primordial soup." The primordial soup theory says, "The first forms of life originated from primitive water bodies on earth, which contained complex organic matter. The organic matter that led to the formation of life is believed to have formed from inorganic (life-less) substances present in the reducing atmosphere of the early earth."[29]

This name seemed very fitting for Primordial's focus

on early-stage entrepreneurs and startups. Plus, the name adds to my childhood affinity for prehistoric scientific theories and nicely ties in with Bronto Software and Jurassic Capital.

I started Primordial Ventures with Jenn Summe in early 2023. Jenn is an ideal partner for Primordial because of her unique background working within early-stage software startups and her more formal training as a recent Duke Fuqua MBA graduate. She can empathize with early-stage entrepreneurs and understand their startup's business models, making her perfect for investing in and supporting them.

We target startups that have less than $1 million in annual sales, including some that are pre-revenue. Like with Jurassic, we have developed an investment model and a range of programs appropriate for this stage of the startup lifecycle. What it takes to get a startup from zero to $1 million in sales differs from what it takes to get a startup from $1 million to $10 million in annual sales. The entrepreneur must "play different games at different times." We believe it and have developed our investment model appropriately.

Compared to Jurassic, Primordial makes more frequent but smaller investments in startups. We strive to invest in one new startup per month. In addition to capital, we provide programming and various other forms of support—including quarterly investor meet-and-greets, founder-only lunches, and monthly guidance sessions to keep them on track.

Community is important for founders. Founder life is often a lonely life. It is hard for other people, even your partner, to understand the trials and tribulations of trying to build a startup. But other founders definitely get it. Primordial's events connect founders who are going through similar entrepreneurial journeys. We also provide coworking space in our building so the founders can work with each other, share ideas, and socialize.

Overall, whether through GrepBeat, Jurassic, or Primordial, Colopy Ventures is designed to give back—to help others follow their entrepreneurial journeys and transform their lives, just like my journey did for me and, in some small way, the many employees and customers of Bronto.

The entrepreneurial life does not have to end when you have graduated your startup. For me, I can pay it forward and help others—much like others helped me. I encourage other entrepreneurs to think about "their next"—and not dream about checking out on life from a beach or sailboat but rather dream about using their entrepreneurial talents to help others.

Figuring out one's next and post-graduation purpose is easier said than done—just like a building startup. But this is something you are well-prepared to do.

EPILOGUE

This book tells *a* story but not *the* story. There are many ways to grow a startup, bootstrapped or not, and the purpose of this book was to highlight bootstrapping a high-growth startup as a possible path. Without a doubt, there are pros and cons. And, for many startups, bootstrapping is the only option. Venture capital funding is geared toward companies with business models that lend themselves to rapid growth with a hefty infusion of capital. Most businesses are not structurally set up for that type of investment.

Weaved through this analysis of the bootstrapped path, there is also a story—a story of Bronto. I co-founded Bronto with Chaz Felix in 2002 and grew it for over fourteen years. It was hard, and we learned a lot along the journey. Another purpose of this book is to share the story of the journey. It is never easy to grow a business, although the after-the-fact articles retelling founder stories in the media might make it seem so in a "poor but cool" way. The starts are rarely linear. As founders retell their Genesis stories, they are smoothed out and cleaned up. Crisper stories make for better stories but are seldom fully accurate.

True entrepreneurs are builders, and the drive to build does not stop once the companies get sold. It is in their blood. At the same time, entrepreneurs often get started because they see a vision for the world around them that is different from the one that exists. At Bronto, that vision was about building a different type of organization—one that was meaningful to our employees and customers. I think we accomplished that and, at the very least, positively impacted a few hundred employees and thousands of customers along the way.

There is a clear message for aspiring entrepreneurs preparing themselves for their journey ahead or existing entrepreneurs struggling with tough decisions and maybe doubting their path. The journey is challenging but rewarding, and there are multiple paths to get there. Funding is a means to an end and not an objective in itself. Maybe it makes sense. Maybe it does not.

Good luck! Keep up the good fight. With enough blood, sweat, and tears, you can build something great enough to pay it forward to the next generation of entrepreneurs who once struggled like you.

As always... Onward!

The Bronto team remained close, years after selling to NetSuite. This is thanks to the strong culture that we built over the years. This group photo is from our first large reunion on June 6, 2019, in Durham.

ACKNOWLEDGEMENTS

I appreciate these distinguished individuals for reading and providing feedback on this book's many drafts.

Karalyn Colopy
Emily Crookston
Chaz Felix
Peter McEntegart
Kevin Mosley
Jennifer Summe

NOTES

1   I wrote a blog post about "My Hustle into Red Hat" in 2016 and imported the original video to YouTube. You can read more about it and watch the video at https://writings.colopy.com/2016/09/29/2016927my-hustle-into-red-hat/.

2   *The New York Times* published a nice article in 1999 that describes the "Friends and Family" share purchase plans around IPOs like the one at Red Hat. Matt Richtel, "Friends and Family Invited When Companies Go Public," *New York Times*, September 19, 1999, https://www.nytimes.com/1999/09/19/business/friends-and-families-invited-when-companies-go-public.html.

3   a16z is a numeronym and abbreviation for the name for Andreesen Horowitz. The sixteen represents the number of letters between the A and Z at the beginning and end of their full name.

4   Marc Andreesen is famously known for being the co-founder of Netscape in the early 1990s. Netscape created the first commercial web browser.

5   *PitchBook–NVCA Venture Monitor (Q2 2022)*, July 13, 2022, https://pitchbook.com/news/reports/q2-2022-pitchbook-nvca-venture-monitor.

6   Akhilesh Ganti, "Distribution Waterfall," Investopedia, updated April 19, 2024, https://www.investopedia.com/terms/d/distribution-waterfall.asp.

7   Greg Iacurci, "Carried Interest Provision Is Cut from Inflation Reduction Act. How This Tax Break Works, and How It Benefits High-Income Taxpayers," CNBC, August 8, 2022, https://www.cnbc.com/2022/08/08/what-carried-interest-is-and-how-it-benefits-high-income-taxpayers.html.

8   "Understanding the Power Law: Do Venture Capitalists Take Enough Risks?," The VC Factory, accessed March 31, 2025, https://thevcfactory.com/power-law-venture-capital/.

9   "From Alibaba to Zynga: 45 of the Best VC Bets of All Time and What We Can Learn From Them," CB Insights, June 9, 2021, https://www.cbinsights.com/research/best-venture-capital-investments/.

10 Caryn Slotsky, "US PE/VC Benchmark Commentary: Calendar Year 2021," Cambridge Associates, August 2022, https://www.cambridgeassociates.com/insight/us-pe-vc-benchmark-commentary-calendar-year-2021/.

11 *Michigan Celebrates Angels: Empowering Entrepreneurs and Their Investors*, Office of the Advocate for Small Business Capital Formation, U.S. Securities and Exchange Commission (May 3, 2022), https://www.sec.gov/files/mi-celebrates-angels-video-briefing.pdf.

12 *Annual Report for Fiscal Year 2021*, Office of the Advocate for Small Business Capital Formation, U.S. Securities and Exchange Commission (2021), https://www.sec.gov/files/2021-oasb-annual-report.pdf.

13 *PitchBook–NVCA Venture Monitor (Q2 2024)*, July 10, 2024, https://pitchbook.com/news/reports/q2-2024-pitchbook-nvca-venture-monitor.

14 Carol M. Kopp, "13 Business Models: Definitions and Examples," Investopedia, updated November 1, 2024, https://www.investopedia.com/terms/b/businessmodel.asp.

15 Ilya Levtov, "How Much Equity Do Founders Have When Their Company IPOs?," Priceonomics, December 8, 2016, https://priceonomics.com/how-much-equity-do-founders-have-when-their/.

16 Ryan Smith, "Why Every Startup Should Bootstrap," *Harvard Business Review*, March 2, 2016, https://hbr.org/2016/03/why-every-startup-should-bootstrap.

17 *Merriam-Webster Dictionary*, "prajna," accessed April 1, 2025, https://www.merriam-webster.com/dictionary/prajna.

18 There was a 2010 remake of *The Karate Kid*, starring Jaden Smith and Jackie Chan. You can skip it. The original is much better. Sometimes, you should leave the classics alone and not mess with a good thing!

19 "The Lean Startup Methodology," The Lean Startup, accessed April 1, 2025, https://theleanstartup.com/principles.

20 Trevor Kienzle, "Should Founders Take the Plunge?," *VC by the Numbers* (blog), Medium, July 30, 2019, https://medium.com/correlation-ventures/should-founders-take-the-plunge-882e4bf40c9.

21 Grace Ueng, "Culture Creation: Bronto's 8," LinkedIn, May 9, 2024, https://www.linkedin.com/pulse/culture-creation-brontos-8-grace-ueng-f7lae/.

22 Corporate development is the group in larger companies that acquires smaller companies. This is different from business development, which is often within the sales organization and is tasked to develop partnerships with other companies.

23 Investment bankers buy and sell companies. This is different from a local retail bank that may help with loans or hold your deposits. Typically, investment bankers are paid very well and hence motivated to help you. But, because of their fee structure, it often is not worth it for them to get involved for transactions that are less than $20 million.

24 Salesforce has grown tremendously since they spoke to us. For fiscal year 2024, Salesforce generated almost $35 billion in revenue.

25 In the startup world, the law of large numbers means that it is very hard to grow at the same rate of growth as you increase your revenue. (i.e., It is harder to grow 30 percent per year when you are generating $10 million per year compared to when you were generating $1 million.)

26 James Chen, "Due Diligence: Types and How to Perform," Investopedia, updated August 31, 2024, https://www.investopedia.com/terms/d/duediligence.asp.

27 Daniel Liberto, "What Is Keiretsu? Definition, How It Works in Business, and Types," Investopedia, updated August 31, 2024, https://www.investopedia.com/terms/k/keiretsu.asp.

28 "About GrepBeat," GrepBeat, accessed April 1, 2025, https://grepbeat.com/about/.

29 Pritha Mandal and Joanne Abramson, "Primordial Soup Theory: Definition & Experiment," Study.com, updated November 21, 2023, https://study.com/learn/lesson/primordial-soup-theory-model.html.